FOUNDATIONS OF MODERN POLITICAL SCIENCE SERIES

Robert A. Dahl, Editor

THE AGE OF IDEOLOGY—POLITICAL THOUGHT, 1750 TO THE PRESENT, Second Edition
by Frederick M. Watkins

THE AMERICAN PARTY SYSTEM AND THE AMERICAN PEOPLE, Second Edition
by Fred I. Greenstein

THE ANALYSIS OF INTERNATIONAL RELATIONS
by Karl W. Deutsch

COMPARATIVE GOVERNMENT
by Dankwart A. Rustow

CONGRESS AND THE PRESIDENCY, Second Edition
by Nelson W. Polsby

INTEREST-GROUPS
by Graham Wootton

JUDICIAL BEHAVIOR
by David J. Danelski

MODERN POLITICAL ANALYSIS, Second Edition
by Robert A. Dahl

PERSPECTIVES IN CONSTITUTIONAL LAW, with Revisions
by Charles L. Black, Jr.

THE POLICY-MAKING PROCESS
by Charles E. Lindblom

POLITICS AND POLICIES IN STATE AND LOCAL GOVERNMENTS
by Herbert Kaufman

PUBLIC ADMINISTRATION
by James W. Fesler

PUBLIC OPINION
by Robert E. Lane and David O. Sears

SYSTEMS OF POLITICAL SCIENCE
by Oran R. Young

READINGS IN AMERICAN POLITICAL BEHAVIOR, Second Edition
edited by Raymond E. Wolfinger

READINGS IN INTERNATIONAL POLITICAL BEHAVIOR
edited by Naomi Rosenbaum

READINGS IN MODERN POLITICAL ANALYSIS
edited by Robert A. Dahl and Deane E. Neubauer

READINGS ON STATE AND LOCAL GOVERNMENT
edited by Irwin N. Gertzog

FOUNDATIONS OF MODERN POLITICAL SCIENCE SERIES

PRENTICE-HALL, INC., Englewood Cliffs, New Jersey

PERSPECTIVES IN CONSTITUTIONAL LAW

with Revisions

CHARLES L. BLACK, JR.

Luce Professor of Jurisprudence

*Member, Faculty of Law
and Department of Political Science*

Yale University

FOUNDATIONS OF MODERN POLITICAL SCIENCE SERIES

Robert A. Dahl, Editor

PERSPECTIVES IN CONSTITUTIONAL LAW, with Revisions
by Charles L. Black, Jr.

Design by John J. Dunleavy

(p)   13-660746-2   (c)   13-660753-5

342
B627p2

PRENTICE-HALL INTERNATIONAL, INC., London
PRENTICE-HALL OF AUSTRALIA, PTY. LTD., Sydney
PRENTICE-HALL OF CANADA, LTD., Toronto
PRENTICE-HALL OF INDIA PRIVATE LTD., New Delhi
PRENTICE-HALL OF JAPAN, INC., Tokyo

Current printing (last number):

10   9   8   7   6   5   4   3   2   1

To Nita Bowman

PREFACE

He who holds in one hand a small volume on constitutional law, written by himself, should clasp a prayerbook in the other. A work of this size, designed to introduce the peculiarly American subject, must answer for sins of omission. It is a book of structure and sample; many whole topics are omitted. In constitutional law, even the rudiments are controversial, but full qualification, with adequate statement of opposing positions, would have made a library and not a short book for the serious beginner. The labyrinth of indebtedness to others cannot be tracked; almost all the ideas herein have been repeatedly discussed by many writers. No text of the Constitution is given; it is readily available everywhere. It should be read with care and imagination before this book is read, and thereafter kept at hand. All these faults are those of brevity. In the affirmative sense, the book aims to give those who come to constitutional law a good first approximation to its shape and workings—to open a small door into a well-furnished mansion.

For this revision, the text has been reworked to include important new developments, without shortening below comprehensibility the basic explanations. Changes are many, but none has been made merely for the sake of change.

Thanks are due to my colleagues, with whom I talk about these matters every day; to Harry Bitner and Arthur Charpentier, past and present Yale Law Librarians, and to the library staff; to Miss Theresa Brennan and the stenographic staff at the Yale Law School, and especially to Mrs. Isabel Poludnewycz, who typed the manuscript, and Mrs. Amelie Gollinger, for never sufficiently to be praised secretarial help throughout the period of revision; to Alfred Goodyear, James Murray, Roger Emblen, Cecil Yarbrough, Wilbur Mangas, and Norma Karlin, all now or formerly at Prentice-Hall, for editorial help; to Meira Pimsleur, for the index; and to Barbara Aronstein Black, for everything.

Charles L. Black, Jr.

New Haven, 1969

CONTENTS

PERSPECTIVES
IN
CONSTITUTIONAL
LAW

THE MAKING OF CONSTITUTIONAL LAW

DOCUMENT AND COURT

The highest interests of constitutional law are enfolded in its name. A "constitution" is a matter of purest politics, a structure of power. "Law" is the machinery—courts and concepts, steel bars and statutes—for dealing with conflict between man and man, and with infractions of public order. The term "constitutional law" symbolizes an intersection of law and politics, wherein issues of political power are acted on by persons trained in the legal tradition, working in judicial institutions, following the procedures of law, thinking as lawyers think.

The supporting theory is well-known. The Constitution is a *superior law*. Our courts (unlike the courts of many countries) apply the Constitution as law to the cases before them. An American court does not enforce a criminal statute which is, in the court's judgment, forbidden by the Constitution. A statute relieving persons from the obligation of a designated sort of contract will not prevent enforcement of such a contract, if the court believes the statute violates the "obligation of contracts" clause in Article I, §10. If the President orders property seized, and a court thinks the Constitution forbids this step, the court will order the property returned.[1] The practical result in each case is that somebody wins his lawsuit. The constitutional grounds relied on, collected and ordered by courts and commentators, make up the body of judicially fashioned constitutional law.

[1] Youngstown Sheet and Tube Co. v. Sawyer, 343 U.S. 579 (1952). In citations to law reports and periodicals, the volume number precedes and the page number follows the name of the series. "U.S." means "United States Reports," the official reports of the Supreme Court; for older decisions, the volume and name of the reporter is first given, with the "U.S." volume in parentheses immediately following.

1

The legitimacy of this judicial practice has been questioned.[2] The Constitution does not in so many words give this function to the courts—any more than it gives Congress the power of investigation. But it does declare that "this Constitution" shall be (along with federal statutes and treaties) the "supreme Law of the Land" (Article VI); this means "law to be used in the decision of cases," because it is added that "the Judges in every State shall be bound thereby. . . ." Unless there is reason (as there is not) for holding state judges bound by the federal Constitution while federal judges are not so bound, the implication is that all judges are to treat the Constitution as law, the state judges being specially mentioned only because there might have been some doubt about them. Article III confirms this by extending the federal judicial power to cases "arising under this Constitution."

If the Constitution is law, it is surely a superior law, outranking ordinary statutes. The Constitution itself speaks in terms that imply this superiority; it says, for example, what laws may and may not be passed by Congress (Article I, §§8–9). It is wrong to say there is no textual basis for judicial review; from text alone, the inference of its legitimacy would be more probable than its contradictory; the textual ground is quite as firm as for many governmental practices of conceded and traditional standing.[3]

History on the whole confirms this judgment. *The Federalist*, the most significant contemporary expounding of the Constitution, develops the idea.[4] Things said at the Constitutional Convention seem consistent with no other hypothesis.[5]

Further validation lies in the acquiescence and help Congress has given to the courts in their exercise of this function (see *infra*, p. 10 ff.). On a decided preponderance of reason and evidence, the courts' passing on constitutionality is fully warranted. It is well to get this clear, because many people cling to the myth that judicial review was thought up by the Supreme Court and put over on the people. This notion (implausible on its face, for the Court at no time had the means of effecting a *coup d'état* against the will and understanding of the rest of the country) may underlie what feeling there is that judicial review is to be barely tolerated, but not used with drive and courage to attain the goals of the Constitution, as one expects the other functions of government to be used.

In Marbury v. Madison (1803),[6] the Supreme Court (using arguments then long familiar) first held that federal statutes might be nullified by the courts on constitutional grounds. The reasons adduced were not all equally convincing; only one was really necessary—that the Constitution, on the evidence of its own text and with (to say the very least) no effective extrinsic impeachment of that evidence, was a superior law.

About the same time, there began judicial review of *state* statutes (and

[2] E.g., Louis B. Boudin, *Government by Judiciary* (New York: Godwin, 1932).
[3] See also Herbert Wechsler, "Toward Neutral Principles of Constitutional Law," in his *Principles, Politics, & Fundamental Law* (Cambridge: Harvard University Press, 1961), pp. 4–15; Charles L. Black, Jr., *The People and the Court* (New York: Macmillan, 1960; paperback edition, Prentice-Hall, 1967), Chapter I.
[4] In No. 78.
[5] Henry M. Hart, Jr., and Herbert Wechsler (eds.), *The Federal Courts and the Federal System* (Brooklyn: Foundation Press, 1953), pp. 14–16.
[6] 1 Cranch (5 U.S.) 137.

other official acts) on federal constitutional grounds. This rested on the same theory as judicial review of acts of Congress—with the addition that the superiority of the federal Constitution to state laws is (if possible) even clearer than its superiority to federal statutes.[7] As a practical matter, the role of the federal Supreme Court as arbiter of the federal constitutionality of state actions is more evidently essential than its role respecting federal statutes; without such a central authority, 50 different versions could develop of the obligation of the states to the national Constitution.

We have spoken only of the law of the federal Constitution, and of judicial review of state and federal laws for their conformity to that Constitution. Each state has a constitution, and the states have generally accepted the doctrine that state statutes shall be struck down if judged to be repugnant to the state constitution.[8] (No state was under federal obligation to follow this practice as to its own constitution; the fact that they did corroborates the conclusion that judicial review was early regarded as a natural inference from the superiority of constitutions as law.) Each state thus has its own local "constitutional law." We will deal here only with federal constitutional law, as applied both to federal and to state acts of government.

DIFFERING PHILOSOPHIES
OF JUDICIAL ACTION

Few lawyers now reject in principle the legitimacy of the courts' judging the constitutionality of laws. Yet there continues a many-phased controversy over the manner in which the courts should perform this function. "Judicial activism" and "judicial passivism" may roughly designate the two camps. Neither has a discipline or an orthodoxy. Still, one can identify main trends in each.

The passivist makes two chief points. Since federal judges are not elected, he sees their nullification of statutes (and other official acts) as non-democratic. And he insists that the judgments made are often judgments of policy, at which judges, trained only in law, are less expert than are the more practically oriented (and sometimes specially skilled) legislative, executive, and administrative officials whose judgments may be overturned. For both these reasons, he sees the function of judicial review as fraught with peril, and hence to be exercised with the greatest restraint.

The judicial passivist may insist on a strong "presumption of constitutionality" for all legislative, executive, and administrative acts. The real issue is as to the strength of this "presumption." Thayer, in his classic statement, urged (at least concerning acts of Congress) that it ought to be so strong as to prevail unless no reasonable man could think the assailed statute constitutional.[9] This rule, although stated in the form of a "presumption," would virtually extinguish judicial review; no statutes really are passed which no

[7] See the Article VI "Supremacy Clause," *infra*, p. 20.
[8] See Edward S. Corwin, *The Doctrine of Judicial Review* (Princeton: Princeton University Press, 1914), note vi.
[9] "The Origin and Scope of the American Doctrine of Constitutional Law," *7 Harvard Law Review* 129, 144 (1893).

reasonable man could believe to be constitutional. No court has consistently or even predominantly acted on this principle.[10]

Now more commonly encountered is a call for "deference" to the legislative branch, or to whatever official may be responsible for the challenged action.[11] Here, again, the question is one of degree. Nobody doubts that some "deference" is owing. Deference, carried far enough, could make of judicial review a mere ritual for celebrating the validity of challenged acts. Today some judicial passivists would carry deference nearly to that point.

The judicial activist replies, first, that democracy is not simple. Our government is not based on the principle that today's majority forthwith gets all it wants. Our Constitution on its face disaffirms that theory, by providing expressly that Congress may not do certain things, whether or not its majorities think them wise. Our government works through many officials at varying distances from the electorate; our Senate is "undemocratic," on any simplistic assumption; second-term Presidents can never answer to the voters;[12] many other officials are by design isolated from elections.

To the judicial process (says the activist), as to other processes in government, are committed the conservation and furtherance of democratic values. The judge's task is to identify those values in the constitutional plan, and to work them into life in the cases that reach him. Tact and wise restraint ought to temper any power, but courage and the acceptance of responsibility have their place too.

Deference to other branches of government is called for in measure. But a mere reflex of deference may fail to make reasonable differentiations. Deference to the judgment of Congress, as expressed in formal law, is not the same as deference to the judgment of a subcommittee of the House of Representatives,[13] or to that of a New York policeman.[14] Deference even to Congress must have its degrees, and seems least justified when the congressional determination is as to the extent of an express prohibition (like those in the Bill of Rights) placed by the Constitution on Congress itself.

As for the greater practical wisdom of political officials (continues the judicial activist), that too is a mixed bag. Controversy today mainly concerns three clusters of problems: racial discrimination, freedom of expression, and fair criminal procedure. As to the third, judges are the best experts we have. As to racial discrimination, it is hard to see how the question of "expertness" enters. (The political judgments in race cases, moreover, are almost always *state* judgments; see the following paragraph.) As to freedom of expression, some weight may be given to the legislative determination of danger attending certain utterances, but often this judgment must perforce be made in the judicial process, if it is to be based, as fairly it must, on the facts of each case. And whether one sees free speech as an "absolute" or not, the wording of the First Amendment hardly suggests wide latitude for legislative judgment.

[10]See Black, *op. cit., supra*, note 3, pp. 192 ff.
[11]See, e.g., Mr. Justice Frankfurter concurring in Dennis v. U.S., 341 U.S. 494 (1951). The case is discussed *infra*, pp. 86–87.
[12]Amendment 22.
[13]Barenblatt v. U.S., 360 U.S. 109 (1959).
[14]Feiner v. N.Y., 340 U.S. 315 (1951).

On this matter of judicial deference to the constitutional judgments of non-judicial officials, the most vital distinction of all is that between the political branches of the national government and those of the states. The federal Constitution is for the benefit of the entire nation and all its people. Its interpretations can fittingly be ascertained only by some authority representing the entire nation. No state body has any business fixing a final interpretation on any part of it in any case. The judicial deference due a state which determines that one of its own laws does not violate the federal Constitution is no more than that owed by an appellate court to a lower court whose judgment is under review. Politeness is observed, but the legal question is decided independently by the appeal court.

This book is written from an "activist" point of view. The judicial power is one of the accredited means by which our nation seeks its goals, including the prime goal, indispensable to political as to personal health, of self-limitation. Intellectual freedom, freedom from irrational discrimination, immunity from unfair administration of law—these (and others similar) are constitutional interests which the Court can protect on ample doctrinal grounds. They often cannot win protection in rough-and-tumble politics. The Supreme Court is more and more finding that its highest institutional role is the guarding of such interests.

THE REQUIREMENT
OF A CONSTITUTIONAL "CASE"

A constitutional question is decided when it has to be, in order to dispose of a case. The boundaries of judicially fashioned constitutional law are thus related to the possibilities of making cases.

Article III makes it basic to the jurisdiction of the federal courts that a genuine "case or controversy" be made out. This imperative constitutional requirement is supplemented by court-devised rules of judicial policy for limiting the scope of constitutional adjudication. It is not always easy to tell whether a dismissal rests on strictly constitutional or on supplementary grounds; the result is the same in either case.

The Court has not always given to this subject the order that might have been desired. But some categories stand out clearly. The Court will not render "advisory" opinions, pronouncing on mere questions, in the absence of a genuine case wherein these questions are raised; it will not settle some of the questions in a controversy, leaving others to be settled elsewhere; it will not make even a binding declaration of the legal merits of an entire controversy in advance of necessity, or of all reasonably possible clarification of the issues. The litigant invoking the judicial process must have an interest of a sort recognized by law. A party can rely on a constitutional claim only when the invoked provision is for the benefit of a class to which he belongs, unless special circumstances impel the Court to a limited relaxation of this rule. These categories will be illustrated here.

The Court very early (1793) replied in the negative when asked whether it would give advisory opinions to the President; it would not pronounce on mere questions, but only on cases permitting of final judicial settlement.[15] In 1792[16] a federal circuit court declined to consider questions of disability pay to veterans, where the result would be to certify to the Secretary of War an amount which he might pay or not, depending on whether he suspected fraud. This function was thought non-judicial; no effective judgment could be awarded.

Muskrat v. U.S. (1911)[17] represented an extreme position. Congress had passed a statute authorizing certain Indians to sue the United States in the Court of Claims "to determine the validity" of certain acts of Congress which, if valid, would diminish their rights in tribal property. The Supreme Court directed the Court of Claims to dismiss the suits, on the ground that no "justiciable" controversy was presented; the success of the Indians in court would not confirm them in any legal "right" but would merely invalidate the statutes in the abstract.

This decision (and others) made some lawyers fear that the Court might strike down one of the most useful of modern procedural devices, the suit for the "declaratory" judgment, authorized for the federal courts by a 1934 statute.[18] In this proceeding the plaintiff asks a binding declaration of his rights, as against the defendant. For example, if a man believes a state statute is unconstitutional, but fears to violate it lest he later be held wrong and jailed, he may sometimes successfully sue state officials for a judicial declaration of unconstitutionality.

In such a suit there is a genuine controversy between adverse parties; legal rights are fixed by the judgment. The Supreme Court, notwithstanding Muskrat v. U.S., approved the declaratory judgment suit as a subject of federal jurisdiction.[19]

This does not mean that a declaration of rights can be had for the asking. In Public Service Commission v. Wycoff Co. (1952),[20] the Court declined to decide whether a company transporting films within Utah was doing so in interstate commerce, and hence would be immune to regulations the state might later impose. Said the Court: "But when the request is not for ultimate determination of rights but for preliminary findings and conclusions intended to fortify the litigant against future regulation, it would be a rare cause in which the relief should be granted."

Questions of the reality of the "controversy," in the declaratory judgment procedure as elsewhere, come down to questions of degree. The judgment in Poe v. Ullman (1961)[21] went far in declining to decide a constitutional issue on the ground that there was no present "controversy." Married couples who desired birth-control advice and a physician who desired to give it sued Connecticut officials for a declaration that the state anti-contraceptive law violated the Constitution. Although the law had twice been re-enacted since 1940, the Court found no sufficient threat of enforcement to justify a decision. Four justices dissented.[22]

[15]See Muskrat v. U.S., 219 U.S. 346 (1911).   [16]See Hayburn's Case, 2 Dallas (2 U.S.) 409.
[17]219 U.S. 346.   [18]Now 28 United States Code §§2201–2202.
[19]Aetna Life Ins. Co. v. Haworth, 300 U.S. 227 (1937).   [20]344 U.S. 237.
[21]367 U.S. 497.   [22]For later developments in birth-control see infra, pp. 9, 80.

These opposing views show the continuing fluid state of this branch of the "real controversy" requirement. This fluidity does not imply that the requirement has no value, for there are many clear cases. Whatever trouble it may give in an obviously distressed area like that of Poe v. Ullman, the requirement serves a useful function. Our courts work within an adversary process. Evidence comes to them through the energy of litigants. They rely on counsel for presenting argument. These processes cannot work except in an atmosphere (to borrow Mr. Justice Frankfurter's perhaps misapplied phrase in Poe v. Ullman) of "exigent adversity." The resources of judicial time and manpower are not so ample as to justify their use in dealing with questions that do not press for settlement. Above all, the judicial power to decide on constitutionality is legitimized solely by the "case" concept; the train of reasoning summarized in the first section of this chapter has no validity outside the ordinary judicial process. The moral authority of the Court must in the long run decline unless it stays within the force-field of the very logic that gives it review power.

Closely connected is the requirement that a controversy have assumed a definite shape, with issues clearly drawn, before a decision on constitutionality can be rendered. In Rescue Army v. Municipal Court of Los Angeles (1947)[23] an officer of the "army" had twice been convicted under a Los Angeles ordinance governing charitable promotions; both convictions had been reversed in the state courts, and the case was now set for a third trial. Claiming the ordinance was unconstitutional, the "army" sought a court order prohibiting further proceedings. The Court found that the state regulatory scheme bristled with problems of construction and application. It was unclear how the statute would apply against the criminal defendant. It could not therefore be determined with any certainty just what constitutional issue pressed for decision. The appeal was accordingly dismissed. The Court referred to a celebrated collection of grounds which it had hitherto used for confining constitutional judgment within its useful field:

> This Court has followed a policy of strict necessity in disposing of constitutional issues. . . .
> The policy . . . has not been limited to jurisdictional determinations. For, in addition, "the Court [has] developed, for its own governance in the cases confessedly within its jurisdiction, a series of rules under which it has avoided passing upon a large part of all the constitutional questions pressed upon it for decision." . . . Constitutional issues affecting legislation will not be determined in friendly, nonadversary proceedings; in advance of the necessity of deciding them; in broader terms than are required by the precise facts to which the ruling is to be applied; if the record presents some other ground upon which the case may be disposed of; at the instance of one who fails to show that he is injured by the statute's operation, or who has availed himself of its benefits, or if a construction of the statute is fairly possible by which the question may be avoided.

The requirement of "standing to sue" draws attention to another aspect

[23]331 U.S. 549.

of the "case or controversy" requirement. A "case or controversy" pre-supposes a material interest, recognized by law, in the plaintiff.

In Frothingham v. Mellon (1923),[24] a federal taxpayer sued to enjoin the expenditure of funds under the Federal Maternity Act. Her sole interest (other than in seeing the reserved powers of the states properly respected, as she viewed the matter) lay in the relationship of her tax payments to the expended money. The Supreme Court turned her away, saying:

> [Her] interest in the moneys of the Treasury—partly realized from tax-ation and partly from other sources—is shared with millions of others; is comparatively minute and indeterminable; and the effect upon the future taxation, of any payment out of the funds, so remote, fluctuating and uncertain, that no basis is afforded for an appeal to the preventive powers of a court of equity.

Major change in the Frothingham rule was effected by the 1968 decision in Flast v. Cohen.[25] The Flast Court held that the "taxpayer" interest, by itself, gave standing to question expenditure of federal funds for partial support of parochial school activities. Frothingham is sought to be distinguished rather than overruled, but the distinctions made seem (with deference) so tenuous and unsatisfactory that the subject of "taxpayer" standing must be said to have been thrown into considerable confusion.

Many states permit suits in their courts by local or state taxpayers, or even by citizens as such, to test the constitutionality of laws. When review of such state court decisions is sought in the Supreme Court of the United States, the question may arise whether the interest which the state held sufficient to create "standing" is sufficient for purposes of federal appellate jurisdiction. The Frothingham opinion states the general rule as it concerns local taxpayers:

> . . . The interest of a taxpayer of a municipality in the application of its moneys is direct and immediate and the remedy by injunction to prevent their misuse is not inappropriate. . . .

This rule was followed without remark in Everson v. Board of Edu-cation (1947),[26] where a local taxpayer was permitted to question public expenditures for buses transporting pupils to parochial schools.

The financial interest of the small taxpayer in a large city in the expendi-ture of municipal funds may seem speculative, but its presence has been insisted on. In Doremus v. Board of Education of Hawthorne (1952),[27] the plaintiffs sued as "citizens and taxpayers," to prevent "Bible reading" in school, on religious freedom grounds. The state court took their case and decided it against them on the merits. But the Supreme Court found no expenditure entailed by the practice and dismissed the appeal.

[24]262 U.S. 447.
[25]392 U.S. 93. Mr. Justice Harlan uttered a powerful and (to this writer) persuasive dissent.
[26]330 U.S. 1.
[27]342 U.S. 429.

A "taxpayer's" suit is often very much like a suit brought by a member of the public as such to enforce what he conceives to be a constitutional norm.[28] Where the person invoking a constitutional right does so entirely in his own personal interest, two sets of factors come into play—the claim of the asserted interest to traditional standing in law, and its weight in terms of actual detriment or benefit.

In Tennessee Electric Power Co. v. Tennessee Valley Authority (1939),[29] suit was brought to enjoin T.V.A. from competing with plaintiffs in the sale of electricity on the ground that this was outside the powers of the federal government. The Supreme Court held that the plaintiffs lacked "standing"; the right not to be competed with is generally unknown to law, and competition could not be made wrongful, *vis à vis* the power companies, merely because it might violate the reserved powers of the states, who were not parties to the suit.

In Tileston v. Ullman (1943),[30] another chapter in the judicial history of Connecticut's birth-control law, a physician sued for a declaration of that law's invalidity, alleging only that it menaced the lives of his patients and so threatened to deprive *them* of life without due process of law, contravening the Fourteenth Amendment. It was held that he had no standing to assert this claim; the harm he complained of was not to himself but to others.[31]

A shade of difference may be seen between this case and Pierce v. Society of Sisters (1925).[32] There a parochial school sued to enjoin the enforcement of a state law requiring all children to attend public school. The Court invalidated the statute on the ground that the liberty of *parents*—not parties to the suit—was infringed (see pp. 77–80, *infra*). But the school at least alleged a tangible interest; it would have no pupils if the statute were enforced. The troublesome question was not whether the school had standing as a *litigant*, but whether it had standing to *rely* on a constitutional guarantee running in favor of others. The case therefore makes a handy bridge from "standing to sue" to "standing to assert a constitutional claim." Where the plaintiff sues on a constitutional claim, his standing to sue and his standing to assert that claim tend to be confused. But when a *defense* is based on a constitutional ground, the problem of standing to assert that ground is isolated, as in Barrows v. Jackson (1953).[33] The white defendant broke a covenant not to sell her house to Negroes; her neighbors sued her for damages. She invoked the rule (see *infra*, p. 99) that enforcement of a racial restrictive covenant violated the Fourteenth Amendment. The plaintiff in turn contended that the white defendant had no "standing" to invoke the Fourteenth Amendment against a discrimination aimed at Negroes. The Supreme Court both conceded the general applicability of this rule and indicated grounds on which exceptions might be allowable:

---

[28]See Louis Jaffe, "Standing to Secure Judicial Review," 74 *Harvard Law Review* 1265, 75 *ib*. 255, esp. 304 (1961).

[29]306 U.S. 118.

[30]318 U.S. 44.

[31]In Griswold v. Conn., 381 U.S. 479 (1965), *infra*, p. 8, the persons attacking the law had been convicted of its violation; "standing" was therefore incontestable.

[32]268 U.S. 510.

[33]346 U.S. 249.

. . . But in the instant case, we are faced with a unique situation in which it is the action of the state *court* which might result in a denial of constitutional rights and in which it would be difficult if not impossible for the persons whose rights are asserted to present their grievances before any court. Under the peculiar circumstances of this case, we believe the reasons which underlie our rule denying standing to raise another's rights, which is only a rule of practice, are outweighed by the need to protect the fundamental rights which would be denied by permitting the damages action to be maintained.

The net effect of these limitations is far from technical. There is usually nobody, for example, who can challenge in court the constitutionality of a federal expenditure; a moment's thought will show what this does to the notion that judicial review implies "judicial supremacy" over all the operations of government.[34] It may or may not "respect" an "establishment of religion" to have chaplains with the armed forces—but who has standing to raise the question? Section 2 of the Fourteenth Amendment is notoriously violated by Congress' failure to decrease the representation of states where the right to vote is denied for any reason other than alienage, minority, and conviction of crime—but how can a "case or controversy," involving parties with "standing," be made?

The negative effect is that the courts, far from being general guardians of the community, are excluded from vast areas of action. The affirmative side is that judicial business, on the whole, deals with real controversy and real hurt. A statute may be "unconstitutional," but this means only that, if the Court is convinced the statute is hurtful to the litigant as well as unconstitutional, and if the dispute is one ripe and suitable for settlement in court, the litigant will be protected. That is a great deal. But it is nothing like "judicial supremacy."

THE COURT SYSTEM
AND THE POWER OF CONGRESS

The relation of the Supreme Court to the President is simple; he appoints its members, "by and with the Advice and Consent of the Senate" (Article II). The Court is thus not self-perpetuating; it stands at one remove from the elective process. The Court's more complex relations with Congress can be understood only when one knows something of the structure of the judicial system.

We can start with the popular conception that the Supreme Court of the United States is uniquely responsible for constitutional decision. This is false if taken to mean that constitutional decision occurs only in the Supreme Court. It is true if taken to mean that the Supreme Court has the last say on every question of federal constitutional law that can be raised in a lawsuit.

In every court, the Constitution is a part of the applicable law. If a man charged with an offense in a city police court contends that for some

[34]This statement is now limited, to an as yet uncertain extent, by the decision in Flast v. Cohen, *supra* at note 25.

reason his conviction would violate the federal Constitution, then it is the duty of the police judge to rule on this claim. On appeal from the conviction, the state appellate court must decide federal constitutional questions that are properly raised. If the defendant in a suit for breach of contract contends that enforcement of the particular contract would offend some federal constitutional provision, the trial court must deal with this question. The Constitution is law; its provisions, as interpreted, are among the rules governing judicial decision, and are superior in authority to other law. This reasoning applies as well to a police court judge, or to a federal district judge, as to the Supreme Court.

The place of the Supreme Court of the United States derives not from any unique relation it enjoys to constitutional law, but from its relations to other courts. These relations, practically speaking, are created by acts of Congress.

We have two systems of courts—federal and state. In Connecticut, for example, there is a United States District Court; from any final judgment of this court (and of the United States District Courts in New York and Vermont) an appeal may be taken to the United States Court of Appeals for the Second Circuit. There are 11 such courts of appeals, each receiving appeals from several District Courts.

In Connecticut, again, there are a number of state courts, organized wholly under state authority. From their judgments appeal may be taken ultimately to the Connecticut Supreme Court.

If in any lower court a federal constitutional question is raised and ruled on, this is a ruling of law; a claim that it is incorrect may be the basis of an appeal. That appeal, if from a federal District Court, will go to a United States Court of Appeals, and if from a lower state court it will ultimately reach (if the litigant persists) the highest state court empowered to decide. The place of the Supreme Court of the United States is therefore precisely to be defined in terms of its relation to (1) the United States Courts of Appeals, and (2) the highest state courts in which decision may be had.

As to the first, the Supreme Court must (on application) review any case decided by a United States Court of Appeals, where the decision is against the federal validity of a state statute. It may, in its own discretion, review any other case decided in one of the United States Courts of Appeals.[35] The obligatory review is called "appeal"; the discretionary review is called "certiorari."

(There are a few exceptional forms of review provided for in special statutes, but in one way or another all federal cases can be reviewed in the Supreme Court.)

As to the state courts, the United States Supreme Court must (on application) review any case in which a state statute has been upheld, in the highest state court, against attack on federal grounds, or in which a federal statute has been held invalid. In its discretion, it may review any other state case *where a federal claim has been ruled on,* including any federal constitutional claim.[36]

Thus the Supreme Court is in a position finally to rule on any federal

[35] 28 United States Code §1254.   [36] 28 United States Code §1257.

constitutional question, wherever it may first have arisen and been decided.

The Supreme Court has been put and kept in this position by Congress. In Article III, the Court is given "appellate Jurisdiction . . . with such Exceptions, and under such Regulations, as the Congress shall make." Congress has broadly exerted these powers.

Congress has at least as full power over the lower federal courts as it has over the Supreme Court. Indeed, it creates them from time to time, under Article III; they have no claim even to existence except under acts of Congress. Creating them, Congress controls their jurisdiction and procedure.

These powers might be used to cripple judicial review. Congress could, for example, withdraw from the appellate jurisdiction of the Supreme Court all (or any designated part of) cases in which constitutional issues were presented. Congress might provide that, within the federal court system, only those constitutional decisions could be appealed which were *adverse* to the constitutionality of a federal statute. This plan could be compounded with provisions for rehearing by all the judges of the particular court wherever (in the District Court or Court of Appeals) any single judge or panel of three had held a federal statute unconstitutional. Under the power to make "regulations," Congress might require unanimity in every federal court, including the Supreme Court, for a holding of unconstitutionality. The procedures for raising a constitutional question might be made cumbersome and onerous.

These are only examples. All in all, Congress could, if it wished, bring virtually to nothing the function of judicial review in the federal courts.

Congress has no such full power over state courts; some have thought that, whatever Congress might do, the function of judicial review would go on there.[37] This view seems to confuse technical justification with political viability. As to review of *state* legislation, the state courts are in the power of the state legislatures (and, where elected, of the state population) just as the federal courts are in the power of Congress. As to review of *federal* legislation by state courts, it seems plain that this political monstrosity would never be acquiesced in. What moral force would reside in the unreviewed decisions of 50 separate local courts on the validity of acts of Congress? And how could Congress or the officials of the federal government be made to obey? It could, moreover, be provided by federal law that any case pending in a state court, in which constitutional challenge had been addressed to an act of Congress, be removable to the United States District Court there and thence go through all the procedural embarrassments set up (as projected above) for similar cases originally arising in the federal judicial system. There is ample precedent for such removal.[38]

A succession of congressional actions such as these could reduce judicial review to insignificance. All these actions, and many others to the same end, would have at the least an arguable constitutional basis; in taking them, Congress would not be acting by brute force and in defiance of the Constitution. The fact that few such actions have been considered seriously, and that none

---

[37]See Hart and Wechsler, *op. cit., supra*, note 5, 339.
[38]E.g., 28 United States Code §1441. See also Bowles v. Willingham, 321 U.S. 503 (1944).

has won passage, is the very thing that makes their possibility important. Nothing so clearly defines the political status of judicial review in a democracy as the fact that Congress might at any time have worried it to death's door. The point is not what we might think about the constitutional merits of any one of these steps; it rather inheres in the unbroken demonstration of congressional unwillingness even to try to hamper a judicial function which sometimes results in overturning Congress' own laws. No explaining away can rob this massive historic fact of its impressiveness.

A single case, Ex parte McCardle,[39] wherein the constitutionality of the post-Civil War military regime in Mississippi was challenged, is in a special sense the exception that proves the rule. In that case, Congress abolished the Supreme Court's jurisdiction over a class of appellate cases to which one suit already docketed and argued in the Court belonged. The Court obeyed, and dismissed the appeal. This congressional action weighs little against the contrary record of going on two centuries. But the Court's action marks the extent of the vulnerability of the judiciary to congressional control, and hence underlines the significance of Congress' never (except for this case and perhaps one or two other ambiguous and minor instances)[40] having tried to employ this power to hamper judicial review even of its own acts.

Congress has acted on judicial review, but affirmatively. As to the review of state court decisions, the picture is clear. In 1789 Congress expressly empowered the Supreme Court to hear any case wherein the highest state court had decided adversely to the constitutionality of a federal statute, or favorably to the federal constitutionality of a state statute, or adversely to any claim of federal right, and to "reverse or affirm" the decision.[41] This statute not only directs the Court, in cases issuing from the state court systems, to judge the federal constitutionality of state statutes; but also, in authorizing the Court to "affirm" a state judgment that has held an act of Congress unconstitutional, it empowers the Court to make this same holding. The statute also rests on the assumption that constitutional adjudication will be going on in the state courts—otherwise there would be no state court judgments of the kinds described. The only thing left to inference is what the First Congress thought about judicial review in the lower *federal* courts. But that is not a difficult inference; no solid ground can be stated for looking on judicial review—even of acts of Congress—as proper in state courts, but improper in federal courts. This statute has, in such substance as is here material, stayed in force since 1789.[42] Other jurisdictional statutes have similarly expressed congressional acquiescence in judicial review.[43]

What is here shown is not merely the ancientness of an institution, nor even acquiescence based on lack of power. Congress has acquiesced when it might have refused to acquiesce, and has even taken positive steps to facilitate the judicial function. This formal public record of nearly two centuries goes far to answer doubts about the place of judicial review (and hence of enforced constitutional law) in democracy.

[39]7 Wall. (74 U.S.) 506 (1869).   [40]See U.S. v. Klein, 13 Wall. (80 U.S.) 128 (1872).
[41]Judiciary Act; 1 Statutes at Large 73, §25.   [42]28 United States Code §1257.
[43]E.g., 28 United States Code §§2281, 2282, 1253.

THE "POLITICAL QUESTION"

Every constitutional question concerns the allocation and exercise of governmental power. No constitutional question therefore fails to be "political." It is surprising, then, to find that from time to time the Court has refused to deal with some constitutional question on the more or less clearly stated ground that it is "political," and hence "non-justiciable"—unsuitable for judicial resolution. It is not surprising that the "political question" category, in this narrower sense, has remained problematic.

Baker v. Carr (1962)[44] (with the cases succeeding it) is of first importance here. The suit in Baker was for relief against inequalities in apportionment of representatives and senators in the Tennessee Legislature. Though the state constitution called for allocation of representatives in proportion to voting population, the legislature had ignored this command. The result was that "37% of the voters . . . elect 20 of the 33 Senators while 40% . . . elect 63 of the 99 members of the House." Tennessee was a "democracy" in the hands of an inexpugnable minority—surely a serious matter. The Tennessee malapportionment was an example of something that existed to a significant degree in most states, with respect both to legislative and to congressional districts.

The complainants contended that these distortions violated the "equal protection" clause of the Fourteenth Amendment. A lower federal court dismissed their complaint, partly on the ground that it presented a "political" question, with which the judiciary could not deal.

The Supreme Court began its discussion of "justiciability" with a review of the whole "political question" doctrine, and found it to have several distinct branches.

First, the Court referred to "sweeping statements to the effect that all questions touching *foreign relations* are political questions." But on examining the cases, it discovered that this statement must be qualified:

> . . . Our cases in this field seem invariably to show a discriminating analysis of the particular question posed. . . . For example, though a court will not ordinarily inquire whether a treaty has been terminated, since on that question "governmental action . . . must be regarded as of controlling importance," if there has been no conclusive "governmental action" then a court can construe a treaty and may find it provides the answer. . . .

Secondly, the question of the date on which a war is to be taken to have ended is usually a "political question," subject to final settlement by Congress or the President, but:

> . . . here too analysis reveals isolable reasons for the presence of political questions, underlying this Court's refusal to review the political

---

[44]369 U.S. 186.

14

departments' determination of when or whether a war has ended. Dominant is the need for finality in the political determination, for emergency's nature demands "a prompt and unhesitating obedience," . . .

Thirdly, the *formal* validity of legislative enactments and constitutional amendments is usually not subject to judicial inquiry.

> . . . But [said the Baker Court] it is not true that courts will never delve into a legislature's records upon such a quest: If the enrolled statute lacks an effective date, a court will not hesitate to seek it in the legislative journals in order to preserve the enactment . . . The political question doctrine, a tool for maintenance of governmental order, will not be so applied as to promote only disorder.

Fourthly, the status of Indian tribes is usually the subject of judicial "deference to the political departments. . . ." But, said the Baker Court:

> . . . Yet, here too, there is no blanket rule. While "It is for [Congress] . . . , and not for the courts, to determine when the true interests of the Indian require his release from [the] condition of tutelage." . . . [I]t is not meant by this that Congress may bring a community or body of people within the range of this power by arbitrarily calling them an Indian tribe. . . .

The Court then summed up on the "political question":

> It is apparent that several formulations which vary slightly according to the settings in which the questions arise may describe a political question, although each has one or more elements which identifies it as essentially a function of the separation of powers. Prominent on the surface of any case held to involve a political question is found a textually demonstrable constitutional commitment of the issue to a coordinate political department; or a lack of judicially discoverable and manageable standards for resolving it; or the impossibility of deciding without an initial policy determination of a kind clearly for nonjudicial discretion; or the impossibility of a court's undertaking independent resolution without expressing lack of the respect due coordinate branches of government; or an unusual need for unquestioning adherence to a political decision already made; or the potentiality of embarrassment from multifarious pronouncements by various departments on one question.

Having thus established the background of the "political question," the Court moved closer to the case before it. It turned to precedents holding that the constitutional guarantee to every state of a "republican form of government" (Article IV, §4) presents a "political question." The leading case was Luther v. Borden (1849).[45] Suit in that case was for "trespass," and the defendants sought to justify their entry into the plaintiff's house on the

---

[45] 7 How. (48 U.S.) 1.

ground that they were peace officers under the legitimate government of Rhode Island. There were then two competing state governments there, and the plaintiff claimed the other government was legitimate. The 1849 Court affirmed a state court judgment rejecting this claim. The Baker Court thus abstracted the reasoning of its predecessor:

> Since "the question relates, altogether, to the constitution and laws of [the] . . . State," the courts of the United States had to follow the state courts' decisions unless there was a federal constitutional ground for overturning them.
>
> No provision of the Constitution could be or had been invoked for this purpose, except Article IV, §4, the Guaranty Clause. Having already noted the absence of standards whereby the choice between governments could be made by a court acting independently, Chief Justice Taney now found further textual and practical reasons for concluding that, if any department of the United States was empowered by the Guaranty Clause to resolve the issue, it was not the Judiciary. . . .
>
> But the only significance that Luther could have for our immediate purposes is in its holding that the Guaranty Clause is not a repository of judicially manageable standards which a court could utilize independently in order to identify a State's lawful government.

Then the Court drew the circle on the Baker case itself:

> A natural beginning is to note whether any of the common characteristics which we have been able to identify and label descriptively are present. We find none: The question here is the consistency of state action with the Federal Constitution. We have no question decided, or to be decided, by a political branch of government coequal with this Court. Nor do we risk embarrassment of our government abroad, or grave disturbance at home if we take issue with Tennessee as to the constitutionality of her action here challenged. Nor need the appellants, in order to succeed in this action, ask the Court to enter upon policy determinations for which judicially manageable standards are lacking. Judicial standards under the Equal Protection Clause are well developed and familiar, and it has been open to courts since the enactment of the Fourteenth Amendment to determine, if on the particular facts they must, that a discrimination reflects *no* policy, but simply arbitrary and capricious action.

But is not "voting" the "political" right *par excellence*? The Court in the Baker case had to consider its precedents. It had felt no hesitation about relieving against racial discrimination in voting, and in the quite recent case of Gomillion v. Lightfoot (1960)[46] had done this even when the racial discrimination was covert, being achieved by so redrawing a municipal boundary as to exclude virtually all Negroes, and no whites, from the city franchise. A somewhat older precedent was Colegrove v. Green,[47] in which the Court had refused relief against congressional districting inequities in Illinois. But the Baker Court correctly noted that (at the most) only 3 of the 7 Justices

[46]364 U.S. 339.   [47]328 U.S. 549 (1946).

sitting in Colegrove v. Green held the presented question "political" and "non-justiciable"; the deciding vote for the judgment of dismissal was on other grounds.

After this review, the Baker Court concluded that the tendered issue was suitable for judicial handling and sent the case back to the District Court for further proceedings.

In the years following Baker, the Court has made more concrete and precise the standards for legislative apportionment which it reads in (or, as some would say, into) the Equal Protection Clause. By Reynolds v. Sims,[48] Lucas v. 44th General Assembly,[49] Wesberry v. Sanders,[50] and other cases, it is now settled that, to pass judicial scrutiny, districts for the election of representatives to both houses of each state legislature, and to the national House of Representatives, must be approximately equal in population. This substantive rule has not seemed well-based, in all its range, to all members of the Court or to all scholars.[51] But there is more (though not total) agreement on the actual holding in Baker v. Carr itself—the holding that the question of the constitutional legality of apportionment is not one which courts cannot handle at all, because of its "political" nature.

Generalization of the "political question" doctrine is virtually impossible. Baker v. Carr illustrates, in itself and in the adduced precedents, that the word "political" in this usage does not bear its ordinary meaning. Long before Baker v. Carr, the courts were dealing with a host of questions "political" in ordinary comprehension. The Baker opinion sums up (above, p. 15) the most significant criteria, as they appear to the present Court, for qualifying an issue as "political" in the present special sense. Weston's view is also helpful:

> In many of these cases the courts in denying their own jurisdiction use the language of "political questions." . . . [C]omparison of the cases shows that they have chiefly in mind that the power relates to a subject usually dealt with by political as contrasted with judicial methods, and *is at one with, or included in, matters unquestionably and unequivocally delegated to the executive and legislative departments.* . . . The process is *interpretative*, and the decisions do not represent a formula for judicial dexterity in avoiding "prickly issues." [Italics supplied.][52]

This way of looking at the matter brings the "political question" doctrine into the intellectual frame of judicial review as a whole. In the "political question" case, the Court is not refusing to decide any relevant question of law, on grounds extrinsic to legality, but is deciding the relevant preliminary legal question—whether, expressly or by fair implication, the Constitution, as a matter of law, bestows final power on some authority other than the Court.

The difference between this intellectual mode and that of perceiving the "political question" doctrine as an amorphous exception to constitu-

---

[48]377 U.S. 533 (1964).   [49]377 U.S. 713 (1964).   [50]376 U.S. 1 (1964).
[51]For an excellent discussion, see Martin Shapiro, *Law and Politics in the Supreme Court* (New York: Free Press, 1964), pp. 174–252.
[52]Melville F. Weston, "Political Questions," 38 *Harvard Law Review* 296 (1925).

tional legality may seem merely aesthetic. If that were true, the shift might still be well, for the exception of "political" questions from a field of decision where all the questions are really "political" is indeed offensive to taste. But there is more to it than that. Our symbolization rules us; a ground of decision which could, as a matter of common meaning, apply to all the presented cases is hard to apply with rational differentiation to those few cases where it has value. It is better to say that the general rule is that all governmental acts are, when brought in issue in regular cases, to be judged for their conformity to the Constitution, except where that instrument itself may—expressly or by fair implication—be taken to have put final power elsewhere. That is all there is to the "political question" doctrine, insofar as it is susceptible of any general statement, and this formulation puts on the one who invokes it the very burden he ought to bear—that of producing satisfactory reasons for the introduction of the claimed exception.

The "political question" matter could, however, be put from another perspective. One could begin from the obvious truth that the great majority of governmental questions are evidently for handling by the legislative and executive branches. All run-of-the-mill questions—the size of appropriations, the amount of the President's salary, the length of terms of Federal Trade Commissioners, the day for celebrating Thanksgiving, the best way to fight a war—are obviously questions of pure policy, having no legal quality whatever, manageable by no legal manipulations. A relatively small (though still large) number of questions are rather obviously judicial—the meaning of the ex *post facto* clause, of the jury trial requirement. There is a borderland, containing questions which might reasonably be looked on as in either category. It falls to the Court to determine whether the issue tendered is one which is fairly to be looked on as one submitted to (and soluble by) the processes of law.

CHAPTER TWO

FEDERALISM AND THE PILLARS OF NATIONAL POWER

THE NATIONAL AUTHORITY

A General View. The national government's power is defined in doctrine (1) by the scope of affirmative grants, such as the clauses giving Congress power over bankruptcy,[1] and giving the President power to receive ambassadors;[2] (2) by the limiting effect of prohibitions on the exercise of the granted powers, such as the one that forbids the passage by Congress of a bill of attainder;[3] and (3) by whatever inferences may be drawn from the structure of the government,[3a] including the fact that the Constitution contemplates the existence of states with powers of their own.

The prohibitions circumscribing national power will be examined in Chapter 6. It is enough for now to say that they limit all the national powers. The legitimacy, for example, of an interstate-commerce regulation is not settled simply by its being shown to concern such commerce; it will still be invalid if it transgresses the guarantee of free expression,[4] or amounts to an *ex post facto* law,[5] or contravenes some other prohibition.

This chapter will place in confrontation the national law-making power and the powers of the states. After a brief look at the skeleton of our federalism, considered as a plan for distributing law-making power, we will consider the two dominating peacetime national powers—the power over interstate and foreign commerce, and the power to tax—as these are read in the light of the "necessary and proper" clause and of the "implied powers" doctrine. We will then ask whether either of these powers is subject to implied limita-

---

[1]Article I, §8.   [2]Article II, §3.   [3]Article I, §9.
[3a]See C. L. Black, Jr., *Structure and Relationship in Constitutional Law* (Baton Rouge: L. S. U. Press, 1969).
[4]Amendment I.   [5]Article I, §9.

tion in the name of state autonomy. We will then turn to a related problem—that of the limitations on state power that have been inferred from the existence of certain national powers. The national commerce power will here serve as the paradigm.

The Law of State and Nation. The defining character of our national political system is that it is "federal"—composed of semi-independent states sometimes called "sovereign," or, more accurately, "quasi-sovereign." Each state (1) has a full-formed structure of government, and (2) is a giver of law concerning events and persons within its jurisdiction.

The national organization, on the other hand, is not an association of states, but a complete government. It acts, through its courts and otherwise, directly on individuals, without recourse to the states.

For every square foot of ground in the United States, then (outside the District of Columbia and a few federal territories and enclaves), there are two governments and two formally complete legal systems. Conflict often occurs. In a general way, conflict between state and federal laws was settled, as it had to be, by the "Supremacy Clause" of Article VI:

> This Constitution, and the Laws of the United States which shall be made in Pursuance thereof; and all Treaties made, or which shall be made, under the Authority of the United States, shall be the supreme Law of the Land; and the Judges in every State shall be bound thereby, any Thing in the Constitution or Laws of any State to the Contrary notwithstanding.

This clause could not settle the multifarious questions of construction which have arisen since it was formulated. Even granting federal supremacy, it is always open to question whether an act of Congress, as a matter of correct intepretation, conflicts with a given state law. These are not questions of constitutional law, but of statutory interpretation. Several sets of constitutional questions are, however, crucial to the demarcation of national and state powers. First, it may be questioned whether some federal law is affirmatively authorized by the Constitution. (For example, it has been contended that the regulation of wages and hours in manufacturing plants was not authorized by the Commerce Clause, on the ground that "manufacturing" is not "commerce."[6]) Secondly, it may be questioned whether a given federal law is forbidden by a prohibition in the Constitution. (For example, a congressional act stopping the salaries of two government employees by name was held to be a forbidden "bill of attainder."[7]) Thirdly, it may be questioned whether some state law contravenes a prohibition in the Constitution. (For example, state laws limiting jury service to whites have been held to infringe the Fourteenth Amendment.[8])

(There is in formal constitutional discourse no such question, concerning the states, as the one asked of the federal government in the first question above, because the states possess general law-making power, subject only to constitutional prohibitions.)

[6]U.S. v. Darby, 312 U.S. 100 (1941).   [7]U.S. v. Lovett, 328 U.S. 303 (1946).
[8]Strauder v. W. Va., 100 U.S. 303 (1880).

Each of these three questions has been asked many times. The sum of the answers defines—and perpetually redefines—the shape of the Union, the contours of federal and state power.

As a whole, the national government has all the powers pertaining to any of its parts. Since the presidential and judicial powers are largely ancillary to and regulated by legislation, the authority of the federal government may be provisionally and approximately equated with the authority of Congress, and "federal" subjects regarded as those with which Congress may deal. The master-text, then, is in Article I, Section 8.

Some of its provisions concern foreign affairs and the military; these can conveniently be passed over for a separate chapter (5). Others are of minor importance[9] by comparison with the three provisions which have chiefly defined internal federal authority—the taxation clause, the commerce clause, and the "necessary and proper" clause:

> The Congress shall have Power To lay and collect Taxes, Duties, Imposts and Excises, to pay the Debts and provide for the common Defence and general Welfare of the United States; . . .
> To regulate Commerce with foreign Nations, and among the several States, and with the Indian Tribes; . . .
> To make all Laws which shall be necessary and proper for carrying into Execution the foregoing Powers, and all other Powers vested by this Constitution in the Government of the United States, or in any Department or Officer thereof.

The "necessary and proper" clause, together with the doctrine of "implied" powers, has deeply suffused the construction of Article I, Section 8. In McCulloch v. Maryland (1819),[10] Maryland had imposed a discriminatory and destructive tax on the Bank of the United States, something a state could not do if the Bank were a validly created federal instrumentality (see Chapter 3). The Constitution gives Congress no express power to form corporations or to charter banks. Marshall's Court first found these powers to lie in implication:

> . . . But there is no phrase in the instrument which . . . excludes incidental or implied powers; . . .
> Although, among the enumerated powers of government, we do not find the word "bank" or "incorporation," we find the great powers to lay and collect taxes; to borrow money; to regulate commerce; to declare and conduct a war; and to raise and support armies and navies. . . .
> The government which has a right to do an act, and has imposed on it the duty of performing that act, must, according to the dictates of reason, be allowed to select the means; . . .

The issue as to the "necessary and proper" clause arose in a way that sounds strange to the modern ear. Counsel for Maryland contended that

---

[9]Powers over bankruptcy, admiralty, patents, coinage, and so on, overlap in great part with those over commerce and taxation, the strategic arms.

[10]4 Wheat. (17 U.S.) 316.

it was actually restrictive of Congress' other powers, limiting the exertion of these to strictly "necessary" means. Marshall rejected this reading; he found in the clause no bar to a wide choice of means to attain congressional ends. He may have seen it also as effecting an expansion of power, as a coefficient to be applied to the named powers. The case was at least read that way, and the "necessary and proper" clause, with the "implied powers" doctrine, has ever since defined the judicial approach to any problem concerning the power of Congress.

(An important note: It is quite maintainable that the most significant federal powers of all are the powers to spend money, to hold property, and to engage in quasi-business activities and in the affirmative fostering of favored enterprises (as, e.g., by building lighthouses or great power dams). In the round, the "standing" requirements we discussed in Chapter I, pp. 7–10, have made it impossible for the constitutional propriety of these activities to come into litigation. Nobody is hurt when a lighthouse is built, unless it be the taxpayer who (as we saw there) has no standing to sue.[11] The result is that assessment of the constitutionality of these activities, mighty as they are, is a matter of political debate rather than of judicially developed law—though the political debate has been greatly influenced by the Court's spacious views of the more easily litigable national powers.)

The Commerce Clause. The national authority has been defined very largely by the interpretation of the commerce clause. In Gibbons v. Ogden (1824)[12] Marshall summed up and gave his Court's authority to a broad reading of this clause; all later developments are implicit in this opinion. New York had conferred on private persons a monopoly of steamboat navigation in her waters. Gibbons violated the monopoly by running his steamboat on the Hudson. He relied on a "coasting licence" from the United States government, which, he contended, constituted an affirmative federal grant to him of the right to navigate in coastal waters. The Supreme Court agreed. Considering whether "navigation" was "commerce," and hence within the federal commerce power, Marshall said:

> . . . Commerce, undoubtedly, is traffic, but it is something more—it is intercourse. It describes the commercial intercourse between nations, and parts of nations, in all its branches. . . .

As to the comprehensiveness of national power over "commerce" so defined, Marshall went on:

> The subject to which the power is next applied, is to commerce "among the several states." The word "among" means intermingled with. A thing which is among others, is intermingled with them. Commerce among the states, cannot stop at the external boundary line of each state, but may be introduced into the interior.

[11]But see the crucial and as yet vague limitation put on this by Flast v. Cohen, *supra*, Chapter 1, note 25.
[12]9 Wheat. (22 U.S.) 1.

Only one limitation was allowed:

> It is not intended to say, that these words comprehend that commerce which is *completely internal*, which is carried on between man and man in a state, or between different parts of the same state, and which does not extend to *or affect* other states. Such a power would be inconvenient, and is certainly unnecessary. Comprehensive as the word "among" is, it may very properly be restricted to that commerce which *concerns* more states than one. . . . The genius and character of the whole government seem to be, that its action is to be applied to all the external concerns of the nation, and *to those internal concerns which affect the states generally*; but not to those which are completely within a particular state, *which do not affect other states*, and with which it is not necessary to interfere, for the purpose of executing some of the general powers of the government. [Italics supplied.]

The assertion of Gibbons v. Ogden was, then, that Congress had regulatory power over a wide range of events, where these in some way involved more states than one. Two remaining lines of inquiry were pursued, chiefly after the Civil War. First, to what extent may congressional power be rested on the *involvement* with interstate commerce of *intrastate* events? Secondly, to what *ends* may Congress use its power over interstate commerce?

In The Daniel Ball (1871),[13] a vessel operating wholly within Michigan failed to procure a federal license required of any vessel transporting passengers or merchandise on "the bays, lakes, rivers, or other navigable waters of the United States." The *Ball* carried some goods that had come (by other carriers) from outside Michigan, and some that were to go (again by other carriers) outside that state. The *Ball*, in modern parlance, was employed in an activity not itself "interstate," but closely connected with "interstate" traffic. The Court held the licensing Act applicable, saying that the ship:

> . . . was employed as an instrument of that commerce; for whenever a commodity has begun to move as an article of trade from one State to another, commerce in that commodity between the States has commenced.

It then went on to answer an objection often taken to such decisions:

> It is said that if the position here asserted be sustained, there is no such thing as the domestic trade of a State; that Congress may take the entire control of the commerce of the country, and extend its regulations to the railroads within a State on which grain or fruit is transported to a distant market.
> We answer that the present case relates to transportation on the navigable waters of the United States, and we are not called upon to express an opinion upon the power of Congress over interstate commerce when carried on by land transportation. And we answer further, that we are unable to draw any clear and distinct line between the

[13]10 Wall. (77 U.S.) 557.

authority of Congress to regulate an agency employed in commerce between the States, when that agency extends through two or more States, and when it is confined in its action entirely within the limits of a single State. . . .

The suggested limitation to water transport was groundless, and duly fell. In Southern Railway Co. v. U.S. (1911)[14] the Federal Safety Appliance Act was held constitutional in its application to railroad cars not themselves engaged in interstate commerce, where these traveled a line which passed interstate. The Court upheld the act ". . . not because Congress possesses any power to regulate intrastate commerce as such, but because its power to regulate interstate commerce is plenary. . . . That is to say, it is no objection to such an exertion of this power that the dangers intended to be avoided arise, in whole or in part, out of matters connected with intrastate commerce."

This principle could have been limited to ships, rolling stock, and other means of transportation, but it was not. In later cases the national power was sustained over a variety of within-state activities that were substantially connected with interstate commerce: stock transfers,[15] boycotts,[16] conspiracies to fix prices,[17] charges in stockyards,[18] the conduct of grain exchanges.[19] There were some anomalous cases not fitting the pattern,[20] but that pattern was plain; and by the early 1920's—long before the constitutional problems of the New Deal—the general trend was well established.[21]

A different problem (the second one listed above) is presented when Congress attempts to regulate within-state activity—whether "commercial" or not, and without inquiry about its economic involvement with "interstate commerce"—by the device of closing interstate channels to those who do not abstain from the activity which Congress wants to prohibit, or comply with regulations set up by Congress. In such a case Congress is acting directly on "interstate commerce"; the questions are of purpose and effect. Champion v. Ames (1903)[22] is the leading case; it is doubtful whether the Court ever decided any cause more significant to federalism.

Congress had banned interstate shipment of lottery tickets. This could have and was intended to have only one effect, the discouragement of lotteries within each state. The vote to uphold the law was 5–4. As often happens, emphasis in the opinion was on points which now seem less crucial (and less debatable) than what we can perceive as the master issue. The Court devoted itself to refuting the arguments that "prohibition" was not "regulation," and that lottery tickets were not "articles of commerce." The really important thing about Champion v. Ames (and neither contemporary nor later commentators missed it) was that Congress, using the commerce

---

[14]222 U.S. 20.   [15]Northern Securities v. U.S., 193 U.S. 197 (1904).
[16]Loewe v. Lawlor, 208 U.S. 274 (1908).   [17]Swift v. U.S., 196 U.S. 375 (1905).
[18]Stafford v. Wallace, 258 U.S. 495 (1922).   [19]Board of Trade v. Olsen, 262 U.S. 1 (1923).
[20]Mr. Justice Jackson names a few of these in Wickard v. Filburn, *infra*, note 48, noting that they were outside the main trend of authority long before 1930. 317 U.S. at 122.
[21]See Robert Stern, "That Commerce Which Concerns More States Than One," 47 *Harvard Law Review* 1335 (1934).
[22]188 U.S. 321.

power, was seeking to control a matter normally within the competence of the states.

Here is one of the most important questions conceivable, with respect to the legal basis of federalism. Is there an *implied* limitation on the federal powers, to the effect that they shall not be used to deal with some matters under state authority? The prevalent modern answer is negative. But the grave corollary is that federalism has no basis in firm constitutional law. The federal powers—over commerce, taxation, the post, the armed forces, the currency, patents and copyrights, maritime affairs, and so on—can be used to coerce *any* result, however "local," unless such an implied limitation exists, and the concept of a *legally defined* federalism, judicially umpired, has then no substance.

The barring of misbranded and adulterated foods and drugs from inter-state shipment was upheld in Hipolite Egg Co. v. U.S. (1911).[23] Motion pictures of prize fights were similarly treated in Weber v. Freed (1915).[24] The right of Congress to prohibit the transportation of women across state lines for immoral purposes was upheld, as to commercialized vice, in Hoke v. U.S. (1913),[25] and as to a single instance of non-commercial "debauchery" (surely the most local of matters, within exclusive state authority if any can be!) in Caminetti v. U.S. (1917).[26] The picture was until 1918 completely consistent. The cases seemed to say with one voice that Congress might make access to interstate commerce conditional on any factors it liked, and might do so for the quite undisguised reason that it wished thereby to regulate matters which otherwise would have been outside its powers. As we shall see below, this doctrinal line was subsequently (and briefly) interrupted, and then resumed.

The Power to Tax. If the commerce power may be used for non-commercial ends, to thrust into the heart of state concerns, other federal powers may be so used. The federal taxing power is wide; the only significant limitation is that a "direct" tax must be apportioned among the states by population.[27] This cannot practicably be done; "direct" taxes are therefore not in fact available to the federal fisc. For a long time, only real property and head-taxes were thought "direct";[28] some expansion in this term's under-standing later took place,[29] but has been stripped of effect by the device of "indirectly" taxing (without apportionment) the same economic interest as the one that cannot practicably be "directly" taxed. For example, a tax on liquor may be "direct," but a tax on the "privilege" of manufacturing, selling, or even possessing liquor is not "direct."[30]

Any tax makes a money payment conditional on certain relations or events. The tax always in some degree discourages entrance into the taxed relation, or occurrence of the taxed event, where these are voluntary. The heavier the tax, the stronger the discouragement. The prohibitory and regu-latory potentialities of taxation are unbounded.

---

[23]220 U.S. 45.   [24]239 U.S. 325.   [25]227 U.S. 308.   [26]242 U.S. 470.
[27]Article I, §9.   [28]Springer v. U.S., 102 U.S. 586, 602 (1880).
[29]See Eisner v. Macomber, 252 U.S. 189 (1920).
[30]See Note, "The Direct Tax Clause and the Federal Gift Tax," 26 *Columbia Law Review* 852 (1926).

The federal taxing power extends to virtually all matters within every state; if this power is not, as a matter of constitutional law, limited by any requirement that it not be used to invade areas of power reserved to the states, then, again, federalism has no genuine legal basis—except in the shadowy formal sense that regulation of local matters must go under the guise of taxation. It is rather more likely than not that that is just where we stand today. As with respect to the similar potentialities in the commerce power, this position stems far back in the Court's conservative days.

A step was taken in Veazie Bank v. Fenno (1869).[31] An act of Congress imposed a 10 per cent tax on state bank notes. Paper money cannot be issued at such a discount; the "tax" was meant to be and was prohibitory. The state banks that issued circulating notes were generally franchised by the state to do so, in implementation of state policy, within an area in which the states had traditionally been free. The Court rejected the argument based on the "reserved rights of the states," which it defined narrowly:

> . . . It may be admitted that the reserved rights of the States, such as the right to pass laws, to give effect to laws through executive action, to administer justice through the courts, and to employ all necessary agencies for legitimate purposes of State government, are not proper subjects of the taxing power of Congress. . . .

The Court might here be taken to imply that Congress, by the formality of "taxation," may prohibit any activity, however interesting or vital to a state, except those having directly to do with the structures of the state government. But the force of the holding is weakened by the proffering of an alternative ground:

> Having . . . in the exercise of undisputed constitutional powers, undertaken to provide a currency for the whole country, it cannot be questioned that Congress may, constitutionally, secure the benefit of it to the people by appropriate legislation. . . . Congress may restrain, by suitable enactments, the circulation as money of any notes not issued under its own authority. . . .

The Veazie decision, then, might be regarded as resting on no more than a broad view of Congress' power over the currency. McCray v. U.S. (1904)[32] cannot be so explained. Congress put a tax of 10 cents a pound on yellow oleomargarine, whether or not its manufacture or sale had any connection with "interstate commerce" or with any other area of federal concern. Oleomargarine carried no such profit; the tax amounted to a prohibition on the manufacture or sale of colored oleomargarine within any state. One of two things is true. Either such a transaction is within the state and not the federal power, or there are no transactions so to be classified. But the Court of 1904 gave forth the pure doctrine:

Undoubtedly, in determining whether a particular act is within a

[31]8 Wall. (75 U.S.) 533.   [32]195 U.S. 27.

granted power, its scope and effect are to be considered. Applying this rule to the acts assailed, it is self-evident that on their face they levy an excise tax. That being their necessary scope and operation, it follows that the acts are within the grant of power. . . .

Since, as pointed out in all the decisions referred to, the taxing power conferred by the Constitution knows no limits except those expressly stated in that instrument, it must follow, if a tax be within the lawful power, the exertion of that power may not be judicially restrained because of the results to arise from its exercise. . . .

In U.S. v. Doremus (1919),[33] a new twist was put on the taxing power. A federal tax on narcotics (trivial in amount) was accompanied by detailed regulations requiring that records be kept and fixed procedures be followed by those in this dreadful trade. The scheme was upheld, the Court refusing to consider that "another motive than taxation, not shown on the face of the act, might have contributed to its passage."

Dagenhart and Drexel: The Court Draws Back. The whole push of doctrine, then, at about the end of World War I, supported three propositions:

1. Congress, besides regulating obviously "interstate" commerce, might regulate matters substantially related to such commerce.[34]
2. Congress might cut off access to the channels of interstate commerce on any basis it pleased, without regard to the consequent (or even the intended) impact on matters primarily under state regulatory power.
3. Congress might use its taxing power, even to the point of prohibition, without reference to any implied limit set by the autonomous law-making power of the states.

This was the position at about the time of the decisions in Hammer v. Dagenhart (1918)[35] and Bailey v. Drexel Furniture Co. (1922).[36] In the Hammer case, Congress had passed a law prohibiting interstate shipment of goods produced in factories that employed children. The Court operated heroically to distinguish the massive precedents, including the lottery, drugs, obscene literature, and prostitution cases: "In each of these instances," it said, "the use of interstate transportation was necessary to the *accomplishment* of harmful results." (Italics supplied.) By contrast, child-made goods were "harmless."

The descriptive accuracy of this distinction is questionable; the competition of child-made goods in states prohibiting child labor might be the evil the "accomplishment" of which Congress was aiming to prevent. But the distinction is in any case not cogent; if Congress may prohibit interstate traffic in order to prevent results it considers "harmful" in the receiving state,

---

[33]249 U.S. 86.
[34]The limits to this principle were quite unclear, the applications various. See above, note 21.
[35]247 U.S. 251.
[36]259 U.S. 20.

however "local" these harms may be, why may it not do the same as to similarly local harms in the sending state? The heart of the opinion lay elsewhere: "In our view, the necessary effect of this act is . . . to regulate the hours of labor of children, . . . a purely state authority." The law was invalidated.

In the Drexel case Congress (after the Hammer ruling) turned to the second pillar of federal power, taxation. A heavy tax was placed on "Employment of Child Labor." Regulations were imposed, defining child labor and providing for inspection. Invalidating this tax, the Court said: ". . . a court must be blind not to see that the so-called tax is imposed to stop the employment of children. . . ."

These two cases reversed the doctrinal trend of 60 years. Justice Holmes dissented in the Hammer case:

> The question, then, is narrowed to whether the exercise of its otherwise constitutional power by Congress can be pronounced unconstitutional because of its possible reaction upon the conduct of the States in a matter upon which I have admitted that they are free from direct control. I should have thought that that matter had been disposed of so fully as to leave no room for doubt. . . .
>
> The act does not meddle with anything belonging to the States. They may regulate their internal affairs and their domestic commerce as they like. But when they seek to send their products across the state line they are no longer within their rights. If there were no Constitution and no Congress their power to cross the line would depend upon their neighbors. Under the Constitution such commerce belongs not to the States but to Congress to regulate. It may carry out its views of public policy whatever indirect effect they may have upon the activities of the States.

Hammer v. Dagenhart has now been overruled,[37] and the older view has resumed its sway. Yet the case posed the key issue of federalism, considered as a legal system. A federal government must be given powers broadly expressed and hence susceptible of great expansion; if this is not done, the federal government will not be a workable structure, adequate to emergent need. Our national commerce and taxing powers are typical; neither text nor context will bear restrictive interpretation.

Given national powers of this extension, one of two things must be true: Either they furnish the federal government with an authentic legal basis for dealing effectively with anything at all, without regard to state autonomy, or they are, as a matter of law, limited by some implied constitutional prohibition against their use in such a manner as to invade areas of power reserved to the states. Working out the contours of such an implied prohibition, if it exists, must be a matter of continuing great difficulty. The categorical issue is whether, within our constitutional logic, such a limitation exists at all.

Holmes, in Hammer, seems to be saying that it does not. As we have seen, there is support in the older cases for this view.

But are not its implications startling? Can Congress prohibit the inter-

[37]United States v. Darby, 312 U.S. 100 (1941).

state travel of divorced men? Such a law would have no close relation to economic matters, but that is true of the Mann Act, as applied to non-commercialized "immorality." Could Congress bar from interstate shipment goods produced in a factory where employees swear? If not, why not? Some people think swearing is worse than child labor; some think it not as bad.

Unless one is prepared to answer these questions in the affirmative, as a matter of constitutional law, one must conclude that some limits on federal power arise by mere implication from the fact of there being states, with general authority over their own local concerns. There is nothing strange to constitutional discourse about an implied limitation on governmental power; the states are subject to disabilities that are merely inferred from the co-existence of the federal government, and there is no reason why an implication might not run the other way.

The issue here is not whether our federal system, with state quasi-sovereignty, has *any* basis. It has a basis in the political structure of the national government. As long as representatives and senators conceive themselves as representing their states, some state independence will remain.[38] The issue, rather, is whether the federal system has any *legal* substance, any core of constitutional right that courts will enforce.

If it has not, but exists only at the sufferance of Congress, that cardinal fact should be recognized. The only viable alternative is the working out of a body of doctrine stating limitations on Congress that are implied from the existence and authority of the states.

(The question has been confused by the fact that discussion of "states' rights" usually centers around the Fourteenth Amendment, which enunciates prohibitions against the states, thereby settling that, in the areas of prohibition, they are to be the reverse of independent. No more ill-chosen terrain can be imagined for a rational defense of states' rights.)

Whose Rights Are States' Rights? Perhaps its frequent "windfall" effect is an obstacle to the working out of a doctrine of federal limitation. A man is indicted for shipping lottery tickets from Texas to California. He seeks to escape on the ground that the law infringes the rights of those (and other) states to regulate their own institutions. But the party in whose favor the implied guarantee of state autonomy runs, if it exists at all, is the state, considered as a polity.[39] Why should the man escape conviction, when, for all we know, all the states involved gladly acquiesce in the federal law? People are sometimes allowed to assert other people's rights;[40] but is the collision of federal and state power a suitable one for conferring this standing on a private person? If federal law infringes state right, ought not the state or states that object be the assertors of the claim?

There is precedent for this. In Missouri v. Holland (1920),[41] the state claimed that the federal Migratory Bird Act invaded both its property (in the

---

[38]See Herbert Wechsler, "The Political Safeguards of Federalism," in his *Principles, Politics & Fundamental Law* (Cambridge: Harvard University Press, 1961), p. 49.

[39]See Tenn. Elec. Power Co. v. T.V.A., 306 U.S. 118 (1939). In South Carolina v. Katzenbach, 383 U.S. 301 (1966), a state was conceded "standing" to contest the validity of the Voting Rights Act of 1965. See *infra*, p. 103.

[40]See *supra*, pp. 9–10.   [41]252 U.S. 416 (1920). (Discussed *infra*, p. 66)

birds, while still unshot) and its sovereign power as a state, over the subject of hunting within its borders. The "property" peg was wobbly. But Holmes said firmly, for a Court unanimous on the point of "standing," though divided on the merits, "it is enough [for "standing"] that the bill [i.e., the pleading field by the state] is a reasonable and proper means to assert the alleged quasisovereign rights of a State."

A later case, Massachusetts v. Mellon (1923),[42] is not to the contrary. It was a companion case to Frothingham v. Mellon, which we discussed on p. 8. Massachusetts sued to enjoin the enforcement of the Federal Maternity Act. The act could not operate at all in Massachusetts without the consent of that state. The holding would seem to be not that a state may not sue to vindicate its "sovereign" rights but that it may not do so when it fails to allege any interference with them.

A real as opposed to a postulated or imaginary state interest might appear in other ways. If a litigant is acting under a definitely ascertainable state law or policy—if, e.g., he is shipping lottery tickets to a state that runs its own lottery, or that has affirmatively authorized church lotteries—the "windfall" objection would vanish. The appearance of an affected state as "friend of the court," informally asserting its own interest, might have the same effect.

Trends are not always irreversible; we may yet see the emergence of a genuine law of federalism. But that law ought to come through the assertion by the states of their own claims to reserved authority. It may be, on the other hand, that federalism has been eroded away by sheer lack of interest on the part of the states in maintaining their independence, except in fields where the Constitution clearly forbids them to be independent. If this is true, then legal doctrine is a futility.

The New Deal Cases and After: The Present State of Doctrine. It may cause surprise that so little has been made here of the cases after the New Deal; it is often thought that they radically expanded national power to regulate commerce, and to regulate by taxation. Much broader *use* has been made of the national powers since 1933. But little if any new constitutional doctrine was really needed to sustain that use; the "constitutional revolution" of the New Deal was a revolution against limitations quite recently devised, or newly resurrected.[43]

In 1935 and 1936 a Court majority invalidated a number of important measures, and expressed views on the federal commerce power which if adhered to would seriously have hampered national dealings with the economy. Two important examples are Railroad Retirement Board v. Alton (1935),[44] holding it outside the power of Congress to set up a pension plan for railroad workers, and Carter v. Carter Coal Co. (1936),[45] denying federal power to regulate wages in the bituminous coal industry. These decisions (and a few others like them) were not in the main line of the Court's prece-

---

[42]262 U.S. 447.

[43]See Robert Stern, "That Commerce Which Concerns More States Than One," 37 *Harvard Law Review* 1335 (1934).

[44]295 U.S. 330.   [45]298 U.S. 238.

dents; they did not represent a "last stand" of traditionalism. Instead, they revived notions long thought rejected. The substantiality of the relations between the regulated practices and interstate commerce—the factor given effect in many prior judgments—was ignored. The swiftly ensuing change in the Court's line was not doctrinally radical, but resumed past orthodoxy.

As a single example, National Labor Relations Board v. Jones and Laughlin (1937)[46] upheld federal power to regulate labor relations in plants in the stream of interstate commerce. The delivery of this judgment contained high drama, for the recently decided Carter Coal case seemed to point to a negative verdict. But there was in fact no clearly formulable difference in principle between this exertion of federal power and many which had long before been approved—the regulation, for example, of stockyard practices, sustained in Stafford v. Wallace (1922).[47]

Some minor reservations may be made. As a matter of degree, it may be that the new Court has given more scope to congressional judgment (regarding the substantiality of the connection between certain intrastate acts and interstate commerce) than the Court of the time of Stafford v. Wallace would have done. A case like Wickard v. Filburn (1942),[48] validating federal regulation of the production of wheat for consumption on the producing farm, goes far. But the reality and substantiality of the relation between the regulated practice and the interstate wheat market are undeniable. It can only be guessed whether the broad language of the older cases would have been applied, by the Court that used it, to the Wickard situation. In the main, this impression of difference of degree arises from the fact that Congress has since 1933 used its commerce power far more broadly than before; the validating opinions of the Court therefore cover more ground. This does not imply that they invoke new doctrine.

In recent times, moreover, the Court has resumed its validation of congressional actions employing the commerce power to bring about noncommercial regulatory results. In Tot v. U.S.,[49] the Federal Firearms Act, making it criminal for a convicted felon to receive a firearm transported in interstate commerce, was upheld. Most important of all has been the use by Congress (in the Civil Rights Act of 1964) of the commerce power as a means of attacking racial discrimination. In Title II of that Act, for example, it was provided that no restaurant either (1) serving or offering to serve interstate travelers, or (2) receiving a substantial part of its supplies from out of state, might refuse service on racial grounds. Though it may be a matter of regret that Congress felt it necessary to use the commerce-clause approach to a matter so deeply moral in its true bearings, such use, as we have seen, was amply supported by legislative and judicial precedents, and was upheld in Heart of Atlanta Motel v. U.S.[50] and in Katzenbach v. McClung.[51]

Mention ought to be made, too (though out of logical order), of the older cases in which the Court struck down acts of Congress regulating economic affairs, on the ground that they offended the "due process of law" guaranty of the Fifth Amendment. These decisions mostly exhibited that last infirmity of legal mind, sheer misreading of social fact, of the actual relation

[46]301 U.S. 1.   [47]258 U.S. 495.   [48]317 U.S. 111.   [49]319 U.S. 463 (1943).
[50]379 U.S. 241 (1964).   [51]379 U.S. 294 (1964).

of the impeached law to the governmental end sought. Functionally, this reservation is minor; in only one case before the New Deal, Adair v. U.S. (1908),[52] did the Court invalidate on "due-process" grounds an act of Congress regulating a significantly wide aspect of the national economy, and this decision was as good as overruled in 1930.[53] It (and a few other federal "due-process" holdings of less general bearing) are chiefly of importance today because of their having provoked a strong and undifferentiated aversion to any judicial interference with legislative judgment, whatever the textual or doctrinal basis. The Court has recently reaffirmed its now long-standing refusal to tamper with economic regulation on "due-process" grounds.[54]

POWERS OF THE STATES
REGARDING FEDERAL MATTERS

Without Congressional Action. Federation quite clearly puts important limitations on the powers of the states. The most obviously necessary of these is the requirement that state laws not conflict with valid national legislation, or with those constitutional provisions placing prohibitions on the states. Some of the latter provisions bar the states from dealing with matters with which the federal government is itself authorized to deal, such as treaty-making, and the levy of import duties (Article I, §10). Some even more significant limitations of the same kind have been held to arise by implication from the existence of a federal power. With the most important of these—that based on the commerce clause—the present section will deal.

The clause is affirmative in form (see p. 51); as to all of commerce "among the several States," and to much of foreign commerce, it confers power to regulate matters within one or more states. A shipment from Dallas to Tulsa involves events in Texas and in Oklahoma. No congressional regulation of the shipment can take effect other than on such events. Thus Congress, in regulating interstate commerce, is regulating intrastate matters, over which the states (absent federal power) would have entire authority.

If Congress legislates on any phase of interstate commerce, inconsistent or interfering state laws are displaced. But what if Congress has not acted? To what extent, if at all, is Texas disabled, *by the commerce clause itself*, from dealing with events in Texas which are at the same time events in interstate commerce, or which affect interstate commerce?

Gibbons v. Ogden (1824),[55] it will be recalled, concerned a state-created steamboat monopoly on New York waters (*supra*, p. 22). The infringer had a federal coasting license, which the Court construed as conferring on him an affirmative federal right to use the waters. Congress, as the Court saw it, had acted, and the inconsistent state law was displaced; thus it was unnecessary to decide whether the commerce clause alone would have excluded New York

---

[52]208 U.S. 161, holding invalid a law that forbade discharge of rail workers for union membership.
[53]T&NORR v. Brotherhood of Railway Clerks, 281 U.S. 548. The Railway Labor Act was upheld. Adair was "distinguished" into insignificance.
[54]Ferguson v. Skrupa, 372 U.S. 726 (1963).   [55]9 Wheat. (22 U.S.) 1.

from "regulating," in its own waters, the right of passage from New Jersey to New York. But the Court clearly sees much in this latter contention:

> It has been contended by the counsel for the appellant, that, as the word "to regulate" implies in its nature, full power over the thing to be regulated, it excludes, necessarily, the action of all others that would perform the same operation on the same thing. . . . There is great force in this argument, and the court is not satisfied that it has been refuted.

In Brown v. Maryland (1827)[56] the Marshall Court invalidated a state tax on the business of selling imported goods. This holding rested in part on the "Export-Import Clause" (Article I, §10), and on the theory that by paying duty the importer had received an affirmative federal grant of the right to sell; the case therefore held nothing clear on the effect of the Commerce Clause alone as a limit on state regulation.

With the passing of Marshall and the decline of the Court from its ultra-nationalism, several state laws were upheld that substantially affected interstate or foreign commerce.[57] But in the Passenger Cases (1849)[58] a deeply divided Court held that a state law taxing alien passengers arriving from foreign countries was invalid. Evidently, the Court had to work out a line between those state laws which were and those which were not at war with the national commerce power. Since Congress did not legislate importantly on interstate commerce until 1887, and the validity of federal laws in the field could not therefore come into question, almost all commerce-clause litigation before the '90's, as well as much of it thereafter, was concerned with the decision of this question, in one fact-situation after another.

The subject received about all the clarification (though very far from all the talk) that doctrine was to give it in the leading case of Cooley v. Board of Wardens (1851).[59] Pennsylvania required incoming vessels (some of which were in foreign and interstate trade) to take local pilots or pay a penalty. Congress clearly could regulate pilotage under the Commerce Clause, but had not done so. Establishing the principle that was to last till now, the Court said that there could be no single answer to the question whether the commerce clause of its own force excludes the states from acting:

> . . . Now the power to regulate commerce, embraces a vast field, containing not only many, but exceedingly various subjects, quite unlike in their nature; *some imperatively demanding a single uniform rule, operating equally on the commerce of the United States in every port; and some like the subject now in question, as imperatively demanding that diversity, which alone can meet the local necessities of navigation.* [Italics supplied.]

Inevitably, decision according to this rule involves the Court in factual economic inquiry. An illustration nearly a hundred years after the Cooley

---

[56]12 Wheat. (25 U.S.) 419.
[57]Mayor of New York v. Miln, 11 Pet. (36 U.S.) 102 (1837); The Licence Cases, 5 How. (46 U.S.) 504 (1847).
[58]7 How. (48 U.S.) 283 (1849).   [59]12 How. (53 U.S.) 299.

case gives the range. Arizona limited train-length by law; was this valid for interstate trains in the absence of federal statute? In Southern Pacific v. Arizona (1945)[60] the Court held that it was not, after deep study of the effect of train-length on crew safety and the movement of trains.

Cases like Cooley and Arizona Train rest on assessment by the Court of the relative weight of state and federal interests, and the importance of nationwide uniformity in regulation of the controverted subject. The Court has sometimes tried to take a more categorical view of state regulations and taxes, to define some things a state is forbidden by the Commerce Clause to do, regardless of the weights of the state and federal interests concerned. The difficulty comes when one tries to describe such cases generally. Two concepts have played leading parts: the concept that a state may not "directly" burden interstate commerce, and the concept that a state may not by its regulations "discriminate" against interstate commerce.

The distinction between the "direct" and the "indirect" burden cannot be given clear general indices of application; decisions have been correspondingly confused and confusing. In the close case (the one that comes to court) the decision whether a burden is "direct" or "indirect" entails evaluating economic facts much like those governing decisions about comparative suitability of uniform and local regulation. The failure of this "test" is (doubtless unconsciously) conceded by Chief Justice Hughes, who equates it with the Cooley criterion:

> The States may not impose direct burdens upon interstate commerce, that is, they may not regulate or restrain that which from its nature should be under the control of the one authority and be free from restriction save as it is governed in the manner that the national legislature constitutionally ordains.[61]

The "discrimination" criterion may have a firmer core of meaning. An overtly discriminatory regulation is easier to spot than is a "direct" burden. But problems arise in connection with the state regulation or tax which does not overtly discriminate against interstate commerce, but which is claimed to have that intent or effect.

Two early cases are illustrative. In Welton v. Missouri (1876)[62] the Court struck down a Missouri law imposing a license tax on peddlers dealing in wares "not the . . . produce . . . of this State. . . ." This law obviously discriminated against out-of-state goods. In Robbins v. Shelby County Taxing District (1887)[63] the law provided that all "drummers; and all persons not having a regularly licensed house of business in the Taxing District" were to pay $10 a week for the privilege of soliciting orders. This law did not on its face discriminate against out-of-state goods or persons. In part, the Court rested its invalidation of the statute on the high ground that interstate commerce "cannot be taxed at all," even without discrimination. Feeling the insufficiency of this—since the tax did not fall with palpable "directness" on

---

[60]325 U.S. 761.   [61]Minnesota v. Blasius, 290 U.S. 1 (1933).   [62]91 U.S. 275.
[63]120 U.S. 489.

interstate commerce as such—the Court proceeds to point to its discriminatory nature, in practical effect:

> It would not be difficult, however, to show that the tax authorized by the State of Tennessee in the present case is discriminative against the merchants and manufacturers of other states. They can only sell their goods in Memphis by the employment of drummers and by means of samples; whilst the merchants and manufacturers of Memphis, having regular licensed houses of business there, have no occasion for such agents, and, if they had, they are not subject to any tax therefor.

In no field of law is a brief treatment more unsatisfactory than in this one. On the one hand, we have the immensely complicated economic systems of the states, composing the interrelated national economy. On the other hand, we have the rich variety of possible state laws—requirements that milk sold in Madison, Wisconsin, be pasteurized within 25 miles of that city;[64] "use" taxes on goods brought into a state (to compensate for their not having paid a sales tax);[65] state regulation of the price of gas sold to industrial users direct from interstate pipelines;[66] attempts by a state to prevent wild game killed within its borders from being shipped out[67]—and hundreds or thousands of others. No set of general concepts has proved apt for managing this material, and it is next to certain that none will.

Still, the Court continues the struggle. In the Bibb case (1959)[68] Illinois required the use of a certain type of rear-fender mudguard on trucks, including those in interstate commerce. In 45 other states, a different sort of mudguard was legal, and in some was required. Frequent stops to change mudguards undoubtedly "burdens" interstate traffic to some extent; on the other hand, each state has a valid interest in highway safety, and some scope of discretion in seeking it. The Court found the "burden" excessive.

It is regrettable that the Court, with its other responsibilities, should have to spend its time on questions so lacking in legal quality, so little amenable to reasoned rule.[69] It would be natural to turn to Congress; what are the powers of Congress in the premises?

When Congress Acts. To what extent, if at all, may Congress empower the states to regulate or otherwise burden some part of interstate commerce when such state action would have been invalid without this permission?

[64] Dean Milk Co. v. Madison, 340 U.S. 349 (1951). See also Polar Ice Cream & Creamery Co. v. Andrews, 375 U.S. 361 (1964).

[65] Henneford v. Silas Mason Co., 300 U.S. 577 (1937).

[66] Panhandle Eastern Pipe Line Co. v. Public Service Commission, 332 U.S. 507 (1947).

[67] Geer v. Conn., 161 U.S. 519 (1896).

[68] Bibb v. Navajo Freight Lines, 359 U.S. 520.

[69] Somewhat different are Edwards v. Calif., 314 U.S. 160 (1941), and Morgan v. Va., 328 U.S. 373 (1946), upsetting, respectively, state laws prohibiting entrance of indigents from other states, and imposing racial segregation on interstate passengers. These holdings, though each might have been reached on more satisfying grounds than the commerce clause, at least eventuate in the assertion of categorical personal rights, rather than in invitations to detailed economic inquiry. Morgan v. Va. is now of no importance, since segregation as a whole is outlawed; see *infra*, p. 98. On Edwards, see *infra*, Chapter 6, note 20.

The classic line starts with Leisy v. Hardin (1890).[70] Iowa prohibited the sale of beer, and provided for its seizure when held for sale. Leisy's beer having been seized, he sued to get it back, on the ground that it was brewed in Illinois, was still in its "original package," and hence (under a rule-of-thumb sometimes employed by the Court) was still in interstate commerce and outside the regulatory power of Iowa. The Supreme Court agreed.

A few months later, Congress enacted that ". . . all . . . intoxicating liquors . . . transported into any State . . . shall upon arrival . . . be subject to . . . the laws of such State. . . ."[71] In the Rahrer case (1891)[72] the Court upheld this law, but later construed it narrowly, for in Rhodes v. Iowa (1898)[73] it held that even under the new act a state might not prohibit the actual transportation of liquor from without, but only its possession and sale after its removal from the hands of the transportation company. This created impossible enforcement problems; Congress acted again, in the Webb-Kenyon Act,[74] this time outlawing the transportation of liquor into prohibition states. Clark Distilling Co. v. Western RR Co. (1917)[75] upheld this seeming "delegation" of power to the states.

These cases involved liquor, a rather special subject, and it was widely questioned whether their principle would be extended. Then it was held that Congress might apply the Webb-Kenyon principle to convict-made goods.[76] And Prudential Insurance Co. v. Benjamin (1946)[77] seems to put the whole matter to rest.

In that case South Carolina laid a tax on out-of-state insurance companies, which was alleged by some of them to be discriminatory against interstate commerce. Assuming this contention to be true, the Court turned to the McCarran Act of 1944,[78] which it interpreted as follows:

> . . . This necessarily was a determination by Congress that state taxes, which in its silence might be held invalid as discriminatory, do not place on interstate insurance business a burden which it is unable generally to bear or should not bear in the competition with local business.

The issue thus became whether Congress might constitutionally permit the states to go so far as to discriminate against interstate commerce; if that was possible, then it would seem Congress had full power over the whole matter. The answer was clear indeed:

> . . . Congress may keep the way open, confine it broadly or closely, or close it entirely, subject only to the restrictions placed upon its authority by other constitutional provisions and the requirement that it shall not invade the domains of action reserved exclusively for the states.
> This broad authority Congress may exercise alone, subject to those limitations, or in conjunction with coordinated action by the states, in which case limitations imposed for the preservation of their powers be-

---

[70]135 U.S. 100.   [71]The Wilson Act, 26 Statutes at Large 313 (1890).   [72]140 U.S. 545.
[73]170 U.S. 412.   [74]37 Statutes at Large 699 (1913).   [75]242 U.S. 311.
[76]Kentucky Whip and Collar Co. v. Ill. Cent. R. Co., 299 U.S. 334 (1937).
[77]328 U.S. 408. Strongly to the same effect: International Shoe Co. v. Wash., 326 U.S. 310 (1945).
[78]59 Statutes at Large 33.

come inoperative and only those designed to forbid action altogether by any power or combination of powers in our governmental system remain effective.

This decision seems finally to settle that Congress may empower the states to legislate or to tax in regard to interstate commerce with no limitations other than those (such as the Bill of Rights) which set bounds to all governmental power.

From the other side, it is plain that Congress may in general exclude the states from acting on anything substantially enough related to interstate commerce to bring it within the federal power at all, whether or not the area is one from which they would, in the absence of congressional action, have been excluded by the commerce clause alone. The only difficulty that arises is one of construction. In the given case, has Congress, by itself acting, intended to exclude the states? It is sometimes inferred, when Congress has rather thoroughly covered some area, that the states are to be taken to be excluded from that whole area—Congress is said to have "preempted" the field. For example, a comprehensive federal statute taxing and regulating the production of something known as "reconstituted butter" was held to preclude state regulation of the same subject although no specific conflict was shown.[79] Whether Congress has preempted a field is a question of statutory interpretation; any preemption decision can be overturned by Congress, in a new statute.

The Present Roles of Court and Congress. The decisions of the judiciary on all the questions we have here discussed are thus interim and tentative. If the Court holds that the commerce clause excludes a state from regulating or taxing some aspect of interstate commerce, Congress can practically reverse that decision by passing a statute opening the field to state power. If the Court holds (as in the Cooley case) that the commerce clause does not of its own force exclude the states from regulating or taxing something within its scope, Congress can nullify that ruling; Congress may tomorrow enact a general pilotage statute, displacing state laws on the subject and depriving Cooley of practical force. If the Court holds that Congress has already done either of these things, or that it has "preempted" or has not "preempted" some field, Congress can by statute reverse that ruling prospectively.

This plenary power of Congress should be the means to partial solution of the Court's difficulties in this field. The questions that present themselves—as the Cooley opinion makes plain, and as every intelligible comment since has recognized—are questions of economic policy pure and simple, questions as to which regulatory pattern is preferable in the circumstances. Courts must deal with policy questions within law, but these questions have no legal savor at all. The Court has had to settle them because no other authority that spoke for the entire nation was doing it. Congress could lighten the Court's load.

---

[79]Cloverleaf Butter Co. v. Patterson, 315 U.S. 148 (1942). This "preemption" effect is not confined to statutes regulating economic affairs; see, e.g., Hines v. Davidowitz, 312 U.S. 52 (1941), invalidating a state's Alien Registration Act.

In some cases a comprehensive statute might help; state taxes (sales, gross receipts, income, and so on) on transactions connected with interstate commerce might be studied and classified, and a code enacted to cover the subject. (In 1959 Congress did this, in part, for taxes on income from interstate commerce, and ordered further studies.[80]) In some fields administrative bodies already in existence might be empowered to regulate some aspect of the problem; the Interstate Commerce Commission is better equipped than the Supreme Court to compare the merits of mudguards. For those problems not susceptible to statutory treatment, and not falling within the expertise of any one agency, a new central tribunal might be created to arbitrate the questions. Of course, administrative determinations on these matters ought to be subject to judicial review, but that review could proceed along narrowed lines; the courts, for example, would have to decide only whether the administrative findings on mudguards were supported by some evidence, and would not have to make a study of mudguards, as it were, from the ground up.

Other patterns might be worked out. Congress has full authority over the whole subject, which is in all its parts supremely suitable for pure legislative and administrative treatment.

[80]73 Statutes at Large 555.

CHAPTER THREE

FEDERAL RELATIONS BETWEEN GOVERNMENTAL STRUCTURES

BETWEEN THE NATION AND THE STATES

The Nature of the Problem. Our dual federal system produces not only different *systems of law*—state and national—prevailing over the same people and territory, but also different *governmental structures*. This chapter focuses on the relations between these structures.

In Tarble's Case[1] the Court thus speaks of the relations between the Union and the states: "There are within the territorial limits of each State two governments, restricted in their spheres of action, but independent of each other, and supreme within their respective spheres."

This conception is a mighty symbol; it projects unity in diversity, local power in the presence of all-pervading national power. No thought, except the thoughts of democracy and freedom, is closer to the soul of our politics. But the concept enwraps a master-problem. Powers that coexist in time and space touch one another,[2] sometimes with great force; the resultant must be worked out in the world.

There are two ways to eliminate the problem of federal-state relations. One of these is today well on the road to scholarly acceptance; the other has shown a resurgence in other quarters.

The second is the theory of state "sovereignty"; in this context, at its extreme, it asserts that state governmental entities, from governors to school boards, are not properly subject to federal control at all, or are subject to such control only by a sort of comity.

The conflict here is between epithet and reality. One need look no further than the Constitution. Under it, federal law is "supreme." State officers must take an oath to support the Constitution. The states may not make treaties

[1] 13 Wall. (80 U.S.) 397 (1872).   [2] As the Tarble opinion proceeds at once to recognize.

or coin money. Their power over foreign (and much other) commerce is at the mercy of Congress. Courts independent of them are to sit within their bounds. Their militia passes under national command when the national government chooses. Any state must submit to any amendment regularly passed. Such arrangements are flatly incompatible with "sovereignty" in any normal usage.

The state sovereignty theory only generates discontent; it cannot be put into practice. Its opposite is the real threat to the federal system. For several decades constitutional logic has found no place for implied limitations on national power, derived not from state sovereignty but from the possession by the states of some distinct standing, peculiar to the American system, between that of the sovereign nation and that of the province. The Tenth Amendment, it has been insisted, never can cut down a valid federal power, since it "reserves" to the states only those powers not delegated to the nation. But it has not been so clearly seen that, apart from the Tenth Amendment, the whole structure of the Constitution may suggest that the states as governmental entities are to possess this semi-independence. In the last chapter we explored the possibility that the law-making powers of the states might set some implied limits on national power, and noted that dominant doctrine is to the contrary; in this chapter we will consider whether the structural autonomy of the states as governments can have such an effect.

More efficient policemen in New York might well be thought a useful adjunct to our greatest port's working, and hence to the nation's foreign commerce; the best way to get them might be to pick them. A tax on the privilege of holding state office, or of entering a state capital, would surely be a "tax, duty, impost, or excise"; the only question would be whether it violated some implied prohibition on the use of the taxing power, just as a "tax" on being a Republican would violate the First Amendment. To reject the thesis that such an implication may have claim to validity is to reject the legal basis of federalism. The Court has not yet made this rejection, but some of its utterances leave one to ask just why a special federal tax on state court-houses as such, or a federally imposed requirement that state governors be approved by Congress, would be invalid.

These two views—seeing the states as sovereign and seeing them as at the sufferance of the nation—both deny the distinctive character of American federalism. That character is not, and perhaps cannot be made, very clear; certainly, it is not simple. Past and current decisions measure the leanings of doctrine.

Federal Regulation of the States. The most obvious collision between state and nation occurs when one government seeks by law or regulation to impose its will on the officers of the other. The national government has often sought to regulate the conduct of state instrumentalities. An interesting pair of cases were decided only about a year apart. In Hopkins Federal Savings and Loan Association v. Cleary (1935),[3] the association was chartered under state law. The majority shareholders moved to dissolve and to reincorporate under a federal law which authorized these steps. The state had not given

---

[3] 296 U.S. 315.

its consent. The Court first clearly held that the federal act, if valid, authorized the change without state consent. It then held that the act, so interpreted, was not constitutional. The association, chartered by the state for a public objective, was a state instrumentality, a "quasi-public institution," with which the federal government could not so deal.

This opinion was delivered by Cardozo for a unanimous Court that included Brandeis and Stone. The holding (as all are supposed to be) was confined to the precise question before the Court. But that does not detract from the point that, only a short time ago, these three friends of federal power, at the time in revolt against what they looked on as the Court's misreading of the "invisible radiations" of the Tenth Amendment, saw no formal invalidity in the doctrine that state semi-autonomy placed some implied limits on federal interference with state instrumentalities.

The opinion sees federal power and state autonomy as functionally related. The federal act is characterized as "an unconstitutional encroachment upon the reserved powers of the states." But further on the Court says: "The destruction of associations established by a state is not an exercise of power *reasonably necessary* for the maintenance by the central government of other associations created by itself in furtherance of kindred ends." (Italics supplied.) Taken together, these assertions express the idea that permissibility of congressional action is a function of its impact on state agencies, but that, on the other hand, the depth with which Congress may be permitted to reach into state institutions is a function of the acuteness of the national need. This is a more subtly accurate way to view the matter than its statement in terms of categorical prohibition. But the important thing is that the holding gives real weight, as a matter of law, to state independence.

About a year later, the Court decided U.S. v. California (1936).[4] The state operated a "belt railroad" which the Court held to be a link in the interstate commerce chain, and hence within the coverage of the Federal Safety Appliance Act, violation of which was charged. The state claimed immunity from federal regulation; the Court now took high ground:

> . . . The sovereign power of the states is necessarily diminished to the extent of the grants of power to the federal government in the Constitution. . . . But there is no such limitation upon the plenary power to regulate commerce. The state can no more deny the power if its exercise has been authorized by Congress than can an individual.

The Hopkins and California cases need not be indistinguishable on their facts. The contrast between them lies rather in their perception of the issue. In Hopkins, state independence is relevant to the defining of federal power. In U.S. v. California the state's interest in its own institutional independence is given no weight; the events concern interstate commerce, and that is that.

In deciding on the constitutionality of the application of federal law

---

[4]297 U.S. 175. For a recent opinion of similar tone, see Maryland v. Wirtz, 392 U.S. 183 (1968), holding that Congress may impose wage and hour standards on state hospitals and schools.

to a state as such, is any consideration at all to be given to the fact that it is a state with which the national government is dealing? A negative answer, to which the recent cases strongly tend, simplifies matters but destroys the legal basis of states' claims to a measure of independence. An affirmative answer would give to the states some authentically constitutional ground to stand on, but would complicate the task of the Court, for it must then make those judgments of weight which courts dislike making, and yet must often make in all fields of law.

Interesting illustration is found in the line of authority having to do with the imposition on state courts of the duty to hear certain cases arising under federal law. The Second Employers Liability Cases (1912)[5] opened this question in its modern form. In the Federal Employers Liability Act (1908),[6] Congress provided that actions under it might be brought in state courts. Some state courts disliked the act (because it changed the common law of personal injury in directions disagreeable to them) and declined to hear these lawsuits. The Supreme Court held that they must hear them where they fell within their general jurisdiction. This principle was more recently applied in Testa v. Katt (1947);[7] Rhode Island's courts were held obligated to hear suits for penalties under federal price-control laws, although those suits were against the declared policy of the state.

If federal authority is unconditionally paramount to state authority, then these cases presented no problem. Congress might reasonably conclude that opening the state courts to some sorts of federal litigation was a "necessary and proper" step in carrying out its powers. The state courts could be ordered to hear cases just as an individual may be ordered to keep income-tax records. But it is doubtful that the Court would hold, or ought to hold, that the same considerations would justify imposing federal duties on the governor of a state,[8] although this "high ground" argument would apply as well to a state executive officer as to a state judge. The reasons for the difference would take us off the high ground of absolute federal authority into the sphere of differentiations. Historically, the use of state courts to hear cases arising under federal law was early expected and practiced. The Constitution declares that the "Judges in every State" shall be bound by federal law; it is a short step from that to saying that they may not dismiss cases because they disapprove of the invoked federal act. The incursion into normal state working is not very deep; state courts routinely hear many cases rooted in federal law.

Recent cases have invariably sustained federal power to impose regulations on states and on transactions to which a state is a party. California's belt-line railway has been held subject to the Federal Railway Labor Act,[9] and her publicly owned waterfront facilities to the Maritime Commission's regulations.[10] Federal price controls were held applicable to the sale by the State of Washington of timber from lands dedicated to the maintenance of the public schools.[11]

[5]223 U.S. 1.
[6]35 Statutes at Large 65.
[7]330 U.S. 386.
[8]See Kentucky v. Dennison, 24 How. (65 U.S.) 66 (1861), discussed *infra*, p. 53.
[9]Calif. v. Taylor, 353 U.S. 553 (1957).
[10]Calif. v. U.S., 320 U.S. 577 (1944).
[11]Case v. Bowles, 327 U.S. 92 (1946).

In any view, some regulatory power of the nation must touch the officers and instruments of the states; the ideal of total independence must *pro tanto* be unrealized. The nation is supreme. But that supremacy is not of Congress but of the Constitution, and need not imply that state autonomy can never be a factor in assessing the constitutionality of a particular action— as in the Hopkins case. If this idea is passing into history, that is not because of any logical necessity.

State Regulation of the National Government. The problem of state regulation of federal officials and transactions cannot be symmetrical with the one just discussed. All agree that a state official may sometimes validly be commanded by federal law to do something contradicting the command of his state's law. The supremacy clause of Article VI makes it inconceivable that the reciprocal relation could ever be approved. Problems of the impingement of state law on federal activities have therefore been on the periphery; the question usually is whether the matter the state wants to regulate is involved enough with the federal governmental structure to immunize it.

In Leslie Miller, Inc. v. Arkansas (1956)[12] a contractor's conviction for bidding on a federal government contract without having taken out a state bidding license was reversed; no such state interference with federal contracts could be permitted. In Public Utilities Commission of California v. U.S. (1958),[13] the Court held that no state could lay down conditions under which common carriers were to contract with the federal government. Still less may states touch the activities of that government itself. In Ohio v. Thomas (1899),[14] the Court freed the governor of a United States soldier's home, who had been charged with violation of state law regulating the service of oleo-margarine. In Johnson v. Maryland (1920)[15] it was even held that the state might not require a mail-truck driver to get a license, and in Mayo v. United States (1943)[16] a Florida fertilizer inspection statute was denied application to material used in the federal soil conservation program.

In the Penn Dairy case (1943),[17] it was held that the state license of a milk dealer could be revoked for his having sold milk to the federal government at below the state minimum price, there being in effect a federal regulation readable as authorizing application of the state pricing rules. In Paul v. U.S. (1963),[18] a slight change in federal regulation produced the opposite effect, immunizing the milk dealer dealing with the federal government from state price control. Here as at so many points, the final say is in Congress.

"Intergovernmental Tax Immunities." A problem close to that of reciprocal regulation is that of reciprocal tax immunity. The doctrine, like so much else, stems (through misunderstanding, in this instance) from Mc-Culloch v. Maryland (1819).[19] In that case, Maryland had imposed a *dis-criminatory* and *destructive* tax on a function of what was held to be a federal agency. Of course such a tax was invalid. No question of general "tax immunity" was really involved. But the facts of the McCulloch case were soon forgotten. In Weston v. Charleston (1829),[20] the Court held invalid the

---

[12]352 U.S. 187.   [13]355 U.S. 534.   [14]173 U.S. 276.   [15]254 U.S. 51.
[16]319 U.S. 441.   [17]318 U.S. 261.   [18]371 U.S. 245.   [19]*Supra*, Chapter 2, note 10.
[20]2 Pet. (27 U.S.) 449.

application of a general property tax to United States bonds owned by the taxpayer. Such a tax was, thought the Court, a tax "on the contract, a tax on the power to borrow money on the credit of the United States." And in Dobbins v. Commissioners of Erie County (1842),[21] the same conclusion was reached concerning a county tax on "offices," assessed on the "office" of the captain of a federal revenue cutter. Such a tax, said the Court, diminished the recompense paid by the government to its officer. The taxes in both these cases were non-discriminatory and non-destructive; they were imposed not on the government or any of its agencies, but on persons who had relations with the government. McCulloch v. Maryland could have been distinguished out of sight. But it was not, and Pandora's Box was open.

The hinges were sprung by the decision in Collector v. Day (1871).[22] In the McCulloch case, Marshall had at least been careful to note that federal immunity from state taxation need not imply reciprocal immunity; not only is the national government supreme, but the states are all represented in its councils, while the national government and people are not represented when one state imposes a tax on federal agencies. The Day case, ignoring this distinction, relieved a state judge from a federal income tax on his salary. The regime of "reciprocal tax immunities" came to flower.

As might be gathered from these cases, the question has not always been to what extent the state and nation might tax one another, in the colloquial sense of that phrase. The state can never directly tax the nation.[23] Early in this century, the Court held that a normal federal tax might be imposed on South Carolina as operator of a state liquor monopoly;[24] in later cases, other state functions of a sort more or less remote from the traditional were held to bring the state directly under the federal taxing power. New York v. U.S. (1946)[25] held the state, as operator of Saratoga Springs, liable for a federal tax on the sale of mineral waters there; members of the Court, in separate opinions, discussed the line between state functions which do and those which do not place the state on the footing of a normal taxpayer. It cannot be said that the line was made clear, but it is clear that there are some traditional state governmental functions concerning which a general tax immunity, on the part of the state itself, exists. As to these areas, and concerning the federal government as a whole, the troublesome questions have been of the form, "Is this taxpayer, who is not the government, or this property, which does not belong to the government, so related to the government that he or it may not be taxed?"

The possibilities are infinite; only trends and examples can be mentioned. After Collector v. Day, the trend of intergovernmental tax immunities (so miscalled) was up. The high water mark was a 1928 decision holding invalid a state tax on royalties from patents and copyrights, on the ground that these were issued by the federal government.[26] This decision was too much, and was in effect overruled in about 4 years.[27] But it really was no

---

[21]16 Pet. (41 U.S.) 435.
[22]11 Wall. (78 U.S.) 113.
[23]Van Brocklin v. Tenn., 117 U.S. 151 (1886).
[24]South Carolina v. U.S., 199 U.S. 437 (1905).
[25]326 U.S. 572.
[26]Long v. Rockwood, 277 U.S. 142.
[27]Fox Film Corp. v. Doyal, 286 U.S. 123 (1932).

more senseless than the classic old cases. To make a state judge pay a normal federal income tax on his salary does, in a sense, "diminish his compensation." But so does a federal excise tax on the liquor he drinks. A vendor sales tax on sales to the government is usually borne by the government in the end as part of its contractor's cost; but so is the tax he pays on his building. Since neither tax is "on" the government, and both "affect" the government, there seems little ground for distinguishing them.

These considerations, with more refinement, began to prevail in the late 'thirties; reciprocal tax immunities have waned.[28] Incomes of state and federal officials are now freely taxable.[29] People who do business with the government, by and large, must pay normal taxes on that business.[30] Congress may confer immunity from state taxation where it desires; this measure may be one Congress deems "necessary and proper" in the circumstances.[31] For obvious reasons, the states cannot take the reciprocal step.

The new position is not without its problems. No tax may be laid "on" either the nation or a state in its governmental capacity, and it is not always easy to say "on" whom a tax is laid. A tax measured by the value of government-owned machinery in the possession of the taxpayer has been struck down,[32] but a tax measured by the value of real estate leased from the United States has been sustained.[33] A state storage tax of six cents a gallon, imposed on a private company storing government-owned gasoline under contract with a federal agency, was sustained,[34] but the Court indicated that if the tanks had been leased to the government, with the private company engaged to perform services in connection therewith, the tax would have been "on" the government and invalid. These and other decisions place sovereign tax immunity on a purely formal basis; economic burden has been explicitly barred as a criterion.

One substantial principle that remains is that the states may not in their tax laws *discriminate* against federal activity. This would seem not to be a matter of sovereign immunity from taxation, but rather to rest on the fact that such a tax is a hostile act, hampering *pro tanto* the federal function.[35] And it may follow, from the nature of the federal system, that the national government would be to some extent barred from discriminating against state activity. These bars, where they exist, must have nothing to do with "legal incidence"; a special state tax only on sales to the federal government would surely be unconstitutional, though its "incidence" might be on the seller. Discrimination is not always so easy to pin down; any particular tax may be viewed in different ways. In Michigan National Bank v. Michigan (1961),[36] the state placed a higher tax on national bank shares than on those of state

[28]See T. R. Powell, "The Waning of Intergovernmental Tax Immunities," 58 *Harvard Law Review* 633 (1945); "The Remnant of Intergovernmental Tax Immunities," *id.* at 757 (1945).

[29]Helvering v. Gerhardt, 304 U.S. 405 (1938); Graves v. New York, 306 U.S. 466 (1939).

[30]Ala. v. King and Boozer, 314 U.S. 1 (1941).

[31]See Carson v. Roane-Anderson Co., 342 U.S. 232 (1952); Cleveland v. U.S., 323 U.S. 329 (1945).

[32]U.S. v. Allegheny County, 322 U.S. 174 (1944).

[33]U.S. v. Detroit, 355 U.S. 466 (1958).

[34]Esso Standard Oil Co. v. Evans, 345 U.S. 495 (1953).

[35]Phillips Chemical Co. v. Dumas Ind. Sch. Dist., 361 U.S. 376 (1960).

[36]365 U.S. 467.

savings and loan associations. Even though a federal statute forbade "discrimination" in the taxing of national bank shares, the Court sustained the tax as non-discriminatory, in part because each national bank share commanded *pro rata* a higher amount of deposited capital than did each savings association share.

It is not easy to identify the practical issues remaining in the field of sovereign immunity from general taxation. This is true especially because a great deal of the money collected in federal taxes comes back to states in the form of subsidy, and this in turn diminishes the states' need for taxes. If the states and the nation could freely tax one another, it is hard to predict what the "balance of payments" position would be. Perhaps it is best to take the Court at its word. Apart from "discrimination" or something like it, the test is now purely formal; what matters is "on" whom the tax falls in legal contemplation, and it matters not who actually pays. Where the test is formal, one may think that the purpose served is formal, and that the present regime of intergovernmental tax immunity is mostly a matter of symbol and etiquette.

Actions by State and Federal Courts. The states and the nation maintain separate court systems, operating on the same persons and property. One of these court systems may seek to act on the other, on the persons and things in litigation before the other, or on the officers of the other government.

The most obvious example of federal court interference with the state judiciary is in the appellate jurisdiction the Supreme Court exercises over state court decisions on points of federal law (pp. 11–12, above). The federal courts may also directly take over and decide some cases that are before the state courts, by removing certain pending cases from state to federal courts. This, again, rests on precisely limited statutory authority.[37]

In no other way does any federal court directly interfere with the state judicial system. But indirect interference may be effective; a suitor before a state court may, for example, be enjoined by a federal court against continuing his state court suit. The potentialities here have never been fully explored, because Congress has always narrowly restricted the issuance of such injunctions.[38] That they may even in limited circumstances be issued demonstrates that no general constitutional objection has prevailed against them. The theory of the injunction is that it is not addressed to the state judge, but commands the litigant to take some step concerning his state court suit.

The same view would obviate any intergovernmental-immunity objection to a state court's issuing an injunction against the prosecution of a federal suit. But the paramount national interest, emphasized by Congress' creation of courts for federal cases, has generally been held to block the use by state courts of any process which could directly or indirectly frustrate that interest.[39]

---

[37]28 United States Code §1441.

[38]Telford Taylor and Everett I. Willis, "The Power of Federal Courts to Enjoin Proceedings in State Courts," 42 *Yale Law Journal* 1169 (1933); 28 United States Code §2283.

[39]McKim v. Voorhies, 7 Cranch (11 U.S.) 279 (1812). See Note, 90 *University of Pennsylvania Law Review* 714 (1942).

The federal courts, by *habeas corpus*, exercise considerable power over state criminal proceedings. This writ is addressed to the jailer or other state official holding the prisoner, and raises the question whether the detention is lawful. It may be unlawful if the state process has seriously violated the prisoner's federal rights. This writ functions as a supplement to the Supreme Court's power to review state convictions after they have been affirmed by the highest state court, relieving that Court of some of the burden, and having certain other procedural advantages.

Federal-state relations are entirely unsymmetrical at this point; state courts have no power to release any federal prisoner on *habeas corpus*.[40] There is good reason for this asymmetry. As a matter of substantive law, a state imprisonment may be invalid on federal grounds; the due-process clause of the Fourteenth Amendment (for example) controls all state criminal proceedings. It is impossible, in our constitutional theory, for a federal conviction to be invalid on state-law grounds (since federal statutes and judicial proceedings are subject only to the federal Constitution), and, although a man wrongly held prior to conviction, or irregularly, under federal authority, might theoretically have a state-created "cause of action" for false imprisonment, the only substantial question in such a case is (usually) whether the imprisonment is authorized as a matter of federal law. It is natural that the authority of courts should follow the contours of substance.

A third possibility of interference by the judiciary of one government with the working of another lies in the issuance of court orders to government officials. The United States government, as a party, may sue a state, while a state may sue the United States only by consent of the latter.[41] In suits brought by private persons, federal courts may (by judicially fashioned theory[42] and by federal statute[43]) enjoin state officers from taking official action that violates federal law, including the Constitution. This jurisdiction is sparingly exercised; the Supreme Court has if anything been too diligent in finding excuses for ordering dismissal or postponement of such suits—but these excuses are lawyers' law, and cannot be gone into here.[44] In theory, again, state courts might enjoin federal officers from official action claimed to be unwarranted by law or Constitution; for reasons cognate with those mentioned above concerning *habeas corpus*, it seems that the practical propriety of such a procedure is at the very least questionable. Curiously, the Supreme Court has not finally closed off the possibility.[45] Cases in which the state courts have been applied to for injunctions against the actions of federal officials under recent civil rights acts have raised the question, but the lower court opinions, unreviewed, leave it generally unsettled.[46] One

---

[40]Ableman v. Booth, 21 How. (62 U.S.) 506 (1859).

[41]La. v. McAdoo, 234 U.S. 627 (1914); U.S. v. Calif., 297 U.S. 175 (1936).

[42]Ex parte Young, 209 U.S. 123 (1908).

[43]28 United States Code §2281.

[44]Dombrowski v. Pfister, 380 U.S. 479 (1965), illustrates the use of federal court injunctions against state officials prosecuting under statutes violative of national constitutional rights.

[45]Brooks v. Dewar, 313 U.S. 354 (1941); Comment, "Limitations on State Judicial Interference with Federal Activities," 51 *Columbia Law Review* 84 (1951).

[46]E.g., Alabama v. Rogers, 187 Federal Supplement 848 (1960), affirmed 285 Federal Reporter (2d) 430 (1961). (Injunction denied.)

court has suggested that such injunctions, though generally impermissible, may be available where the alleged wrong committed by the federal official consists in a failure to obey state law, in some respect in which Congress has made state law binding.[47] In any event, all such applications, even if originally made in state courts, may be removed to federal court under statutory authority.[48]

It is in the contemplation of our judicial system that any federal claim may ultimately be decided by a federal court (*supra*, p. 11). Normally, then, questions about state freedom from federal judicial interference, or about the reciprocal federal freedom, are questions about *when* and not about *whether* the federal judicial power will have its paramount say. No issue of ultimate constitutional principle is involved. Prudential reasons suggest that it will sometimes prove handy to permit early intervention by the courts representing the paramount federal authority, and normally unhandy to permit the courts representing the subordinate state authority to intervene in the workings of the national government.

Federal-State Cooperation. Federal-state relations have too often been seen solely in terms of conflict. There has always been cooperation as well.

The simplest form of cooperation is consent; consent has worked both ways. There sometimes has been reluctance to permit either of the "sovereigns" to consent to the other's doing anything that might not be done without consent, though it would seem plain that one way of exercising power is to agree not to insist on one's rights. Two bankruptcy cases, involving local governmental subdivisions, are interesting in this respect. In Ashton v. Cameron County Water Improvement District (1936)[49] the Court struck down a federal law providing bankruptcy relief for such subdivisions, saying that this unduly "interfered" with an organ of the state. The state concerned had by law authorized its subdivisions to go into bankruptcy under the Act; it seems ridiculous to use the concept of deference to state "sovereignty" as the ground for thwarting the expressed will of the state. Two years later, in U.S. v. Bekins (1938),[50] the Court upheld a new federal provision for such proceedings, stressing that the state had consented, and politely ignoring the fact that this had also been true in the Ashton case. The Bekins language sets a new tone: "The State acts in aid, and not in derogation, of its sovereign powers."

Consent may run the other way. Congress may waive federal tax immunities. It may, as we have seen elsewhere,[51] permit the states to regulate matters from which, in the silence of Congress, they have been held excluded by the Commerce Clause. It may permit state regulations to apply directly in federal enclaves.[52]

Accommodations more complex than simple consent are now fully sanctioned. The 1937 Steward Machine case,[53] upholding certain of the

[47]Perez v. Rhiddlehoover, 247 Federal Supplement 65 (1965).
[48]28 United States Code 1442.
[49]298 U.S. 513.
[50]304 U.S. 27.
[51]*Supra*, pp. 35–37.
[52]Omaechevarria v. Idaho, 246 U.S. 343 (1918).
[53]Steward Machine Co. v. Davis, 301 U.S. 548.

federal social-security laws, revealed a complex pattern. The federal government imposed an employment tax, most of which was forgiven if the employer's state itself imposed such a tax and set up an unemployment insurance plan meeting federal requirements. The state complied, and seemed content, but an employer-taxpayer objected, on multiple grounds including alleged state surrender of sovereignty under duress. The Court viewed the matter in another light. The unemployment problem had both local and national aspects. No constitutional doctrine impeded a mixed cooperative solution.

Adaptation may proceed by adoption, as well as by cooperation. The national bankruptcy statute makes the exempt property of the bankrupt co-extensive with property exempt from execution under state judgments.[54] The federal Assimilative Crimes Act provides that in federal enclaves (post offices, navy yards, and the like) those actions shall be criminal which are so by the law of the state in which the enclave is located.[55]

The States in Federalism. Our federalism is *sui generis*. Analysis in terms of "sovereignty," as elsewhere conceived, is useless. If, on the other hand, any state claim to independence is automatically rejected whenever it appears that there is some federal interest in the subject-matter, then we do not, as a matter of constitutional law, have a federal system.

This latter point has been clouded by excessive claims of state independence. As we have seen, it has sometimes been asserted that the states are not allowed but required to be independent to some foreordained degree, that they may not cooperate with the nation, that their rights must be insisted on for them by the courts, in the face of their own express desires. Secondly, language of the Court has sometimes suggested that states' rights are fixed in the face of national need, that what is "reserved" to them is in no sense a function of national exigence; this reduces a problem of delicate accommodation to one of blunt (though not well-defined) categories, and ignores the sound technical possibility that a reservation by structural implication may itself be defined, as a matter of law, in terms of the purposes for which the structure exists, and hence in terms of its quest after those purposes in the changing world. Thirdly, the states'-rights propaganda has centered on Fourteenth Amendment questions, a field in which it plainly can make no way (see *supra*, p. 29).

BETWEEN THE SISTER STATES

The Textual Bases. Each state in a federal union maintains standing as a government and as a juristic person. Federalism therefore inherently contains the problem of the states' relations with one another.

Some of the issues were foreseen by the Framers. Sections 1 and 2 of Article IV (the so-called "Federal Article") speak to several problems:

SECTION 1. Full Faith and Credit shall be given in each State to the public Acts, Records, and judicial Proceedings of every other State. And

---

[54]11 United States Code §24.   [55]See U.S. v. Sharpnack, 355 U.S. 286 (1958).

the Congress may by general Laws prescribe the Manner in which such Acts, Records and Proceedings shall be proved, and the Effect thereof.
SECTION 2. The Citizens of each State shall be entitled to all Privileges and Immunities of Citizens in the several States.
A Person charged in any State with Treason, Felony, or other Crime, who shall flee from Justice, and be found in another State, shall on Demand of the executive Authority of the State from which he fled, be delivered up, to be removed to the State having Jurisdiction of the Crime.

In Article I, Section 10, important limitations were placed on the states; the following deals with their mutual relations:

No State shall, without the Consent of Congress, . . . enter into any Agreement or Compact with another State, or with a foreign Power, or engage in War, unless actually invaded, or in such imminent Danger as will not admit of delay.

In the Judiciary Article (III) is a provision which could become a means of settling interstate conflict:

SECTION 2. The judicial Power shall extend . . . to Controversies between two or more States . . .
In all Cases . . . in which a State shall be Party, the supreme Court shall have original jurisdiction. . . .

"Full Faith and Credit." The "full faith and credit" clause of Article IV restates (and makes binding) practices which generally prevail between separate countries. All countries keep public records; the record of a marriage in one country will normally be taken in a second country as evidence of the marriage. All countries have statutes; if two people are litigating in the court of one country, and one of them relies on a right claimed under the statute of a second country, the court will normally accept that statute as stating the applicable law, if the rights of the parties were, at the material time, subject to the laws of the country in which the statute prevails. (If an American, for example, were sued in America for an automobile accident which occurred while he was in Britain, the American court would evaluate his conduct in the light of the British rule that requires driving on the left; would that all examples were as simple!) All countries have courts which decide lawsuits; if, after losing in the courts of one country, a person tries to relitigate the matter in the courts of another, the normal practice is to hold him "bound by the judgment" in the first country, and to refuse to let him have a second day in court.
The full faith and credit clause transforms these rules of international comity into constitutional obligations on the states; the Supreme Court interprets them and enforces compliance. The subject is particularly one of lawyers' law, since the "full faith and credit" doctrines work out into rules of evidence, rules of the choice of applicable law, and rules as to the binding effect of judgments. It is sufficient here to note that the technical doubts are

on the edges. In its over-all political working, the full faith and credit clause goes far toward assuring the citizen of the United States that what is a matter of firm public record in one state will be so treated in another.

Interstate Agreements. The "compacts" clause (*supra*, p. 50) furnishes an adaptable means for handling interstate relations. The states may not enter into any "treaty, alliance or confederation" with a foreign state, but may (by clear implication) enter into compacts or agreements with one another (or with foreign powers) if Congress consents. Permission has never been sought for a "compact or agreement" with a foreign power; it has never been important to decide, therefore, which arrangements would be "treaties, alliances or confederations" (forbidden with or without consent) and which are mere "compacts or agreements." The states have sought and received permission from Congress for many of the latter, as among themselves.

Sometimes Congress gives its general consent, in advance, to compacts of a specified class. In 1934, for example, Congress authorized "any two or more states" to make compacts for crime prevention and for "the enforcement of their respective criminal laws and policies. . . ."[56] An Interstate Compact for the Supervision of Parolees and Probationers resulted. More common, perhaps, is the single compact approved specially by Congress.

A good example of the interstate compact at its most adaptable and useful is found in West Virginia v. Sims (1951).[57] Pollution in the Ohio River could not be dealt with by any one state, but it had not that fully national bearing which made it obvious that Congress should deal with it. Said Mr. Justice Frankfurter:

> Control of pollution in interstate streams might, on occasion, be an appropriate subject for national legislation. . . . But, with prescience, the Framers left the States free to settle regional controversies in diverse ways. . . .
> The growing interdependence of regional interests, calling for regional adjustments, has brought extensive use of compacts. A compact is more than a supple device for dealing with interests confined within a region. That it is also a means of safeguarding the national interest is well illustrated in the Compact now under review. Not only was congressional consent required, as for all compacts; direct participation by the Federal Government was provided in the President's appointment of three members of the Compact Commission. . . .

In the very case, West Virginia was seeking to withdraw from the compact. Of the Court's function in case of dispute, Mr. Justice Frankfurter said further:

> But a compact is after all a legal document. Though the circumstances of its drafting are likely to assure great care and deliberation, all avoidance of disputes as to scope and meaning is not within human gift. Just as this Court has power to settle disputes between States where

there is no compact, it must have final power to pass upon the meaning and validity of compacts.

The formal assent of Congress is obtained to most important interstate compacts. Question may arise, however, whether a particular arrangement is of the sort requiring such assent, and whether (if it is) the requisite consent has informally been given. In Virginia v. Tennessee (1893),[58] Virginia sued in the Supreme Court, asking that Court to establish the "true" boundary between herself and Tennessee. Tennessee answered that this had already been bindingly established; by agreement, in 1801, the states had appointed commissioners, and both their legislatures had in 1803 confirmed the findings of the commissioners. Virginia contended that the agreement to appoint commissioners, and the acquiescence in their findings, constituted a "compact or agreement," void because the consent of Congress had never been obtained. The Court made out the requisite "consent" in Congress' subsequent recognitions of the agreed-on boundary. But it was also held that the pact itself was not of a sort requiring consent, since it did not affect the "political influence of either state." This qualification on the compacts clause is judge-made; but the Court was probably right in thinking that some insignificant agreements between states are beneath attention as far as the compacts clause is concerned. The net result of the holding is that (in view of the vagueness of the line drawn between interstate pacts which must and those which need not have Congressional approval) the part of prudence is always for the contracting states to obtain that consent, and this procedure is followed in important affairs. On the other hand, if this were to be omitted by negligence or chance, the criteria stated in Virginia v. Tennessee give the Court an avenue of escape from the harsh result of declaring void some insignificant contractual arrangement between two states.

The compacts clause furnishes a flexible instrument for dealing with regional problems; compacts not only may settle single issues, but also may set up working arrangements involving the use of agencies having a measure of governmental power, granted by the states jointly. The national interest is amply protected by the requirement of congressional approval. On the whole, the interstate compact is relatively free from problems, and has achieved impressive results.

Interstate Reciprocity. Another mode of dealing with interstate problems does not require congressional consent, because no agreement is made; reciprocal arrangements are put in effect for reasons of each state's self-interest. For example, one way in which the independence of the states has hampered the administration of justice arises from the inability of a state to order attendance in its courts of witnesses found in another state. This has been partly handled by a "uniform reciprocal law," adopted by a majority of the states. Each state, by the adoption of this law, authorizes its own courts, on compliance with certain procedural conditions, to deliver a requested witness to an officer of the requesting state if that state has also put in force

[58]148 U.S. 503.

such a statute. No state is obligated, by compact or otherwise, to adopt or to maintain such an arrangement; expectation of reciprocity is the motive.[59]

"Extradition"—the delivering up by one state of a fugitive from another —also depends in practice on reciprocity. The extradition obligation has a curious history. The Constitution places on the state of refuge an obligation to re-deliver on demand any person "charged . . . with Treason, Felony, or other Crime . . ." in the demanding state. A federal statute of 1793 reinforced this provision by imposing a "duty" on state governors to comply. In Kentucky v. Dennison (1861)[60] Kentucky asked that the governor of Ohio be ordered to deliver a fugitive. (The crime charged—"assisting a slave to escape"—had not appealed to him as a ground for sending a man back to Kentucky.) The Supreme Court, speaking through Mr. Chief Justice Taney, rejected the reasons proferred by Dennison for his failure to act, and declared that he was under a clear duty to give up the fugitive—but held this duty was only "moral," unenforceable by judicial process. Ever since, extradition has been treated as resting within the discretion of the state of refuge.

The interstate "privileges and immunities" clause (*supra*, p. 50) may handily be treated as dealing with an aspect of interstate reciprocity, though here the reciprocity is a legal obligation. It is to be carefully distinguished from the "privileges and immunities" clause of the Fourteenth Amendment. The latter clause, as we shall see, has (rightly or not) been so construed as to mean nothing (*infra*, p. 81). The clause of Article IV, with which we are here concerned, has been given some content. In Corfield v. Coryell (1823),[61] Circuit Justice Washington, sitting in a lower federal court, construed it spaciously to protect:

> . . . [T]hose privileges and immunities which are, in their nature, fundamental; which belong, of right, to the citizens of all free governments; and which have, at all times, been enjoyed by the citizens of the several states which compose this Union, from the time of their becoming free, independent, and sovereign.

(In the case itself, the concrete question was whether a state might deny to a non-resident the right to take local oysters; this was held permissible, since the oysters *in situ* were a species of "property" held in trust by the state for the benefit of its own residents.)

The quoted passage seemed to foreshadow ample federal protection of "fundamental rights." If this interpretation had been adhered to, the clause would have done much more than mediate smooth interstate relations; it would have constituted a sort of federal "bill of rights" of uncertain scope, running against the states. It was not adhered to; the clause has since been given the more restricted but still important office of forbidding discrimination by a state against citizens of other states, except where the fact of local citizenship is a reasonable ground for such discrimination. A fairly recent illustrative case is Toomer v. Witsell (1948).[62] Georgia shrimp fishermen sued to enjoin the enforcement of South Carolina laws regulating shrimp-fishing

---

[59]See New York v. O'Neill, 359 U.S. 1 (1959), upholding one of these laws.
[60]24 How. (65 U.S.) 66.   [61]6 Federal Cases 546 (No. 3230).   [62]334 U.S. 385.

off the latter state's shores; these laws subjected non-residents to special rules and exactions, to the point of practically prohibiting their fishing in South Carolina waters. The Court held these laws invalid.

This clause protects many practices which we regard as normal corollaries of our being one people. No state may bar non-citizens from access to its courts, prohibit their doing business within its bounds, forbid marriage of its citizens with non-citizens; on the other hand, some restrictions have been justified on the ground that some special and reasonable connection with non-citizenship appeared. The clearest example is the unquestioned power of a state to limit voting to its own citizens.

In Paul v. Virginia (1868)[63] Justice Field attributed to this clause a powerful effect: ". . . It has been justly said that no provision in the Constitution has tended so strongly to constitute the citizens of the United States one people as this."

More probably, the clause has reinforced and policed the periphery of institutions that maintain their strength for reasons of more a substantial than a textual kind. It forbids discrimination on sheer grounds of non-citizenship in the state, a thing alien to our thought. Judicial interpretation has pretty much followed the contours of common expectation; it is not to be known which is cause and which effect.

[63]8 Wall. (75 U.S.) 168.

CHAPTER FOUR

THE PRESIDENT AND CONGRESS

TEXT AND ACTUALITY

Questions of presidential power that reach the Court most often take the form of questions about the President's power in relation to that of Congress. The most important aspect of the Court's dealings with presidential power, therefore, is its handling of issues involving this relation.

Surveying the development of the American Presidency to its modern place of symbolic primacy and solid might, against the background of the meager textual provisions in which it is rooted, one is tempted to reject the now hackneyed metaphor that likens the Constitution to a ground-plan, to a rough sketch that left to history the filling in of details. The constitutional foundation of the Presidency is far from having the specificity of a ground-plan, however rough. It was, rather, a starting-place from which the office might have gone down one of several roads. Court-molded law has not been the main force behind the actual development; it has given judicial legitimation, and some legal channeling, to political fact.

The textual matter about the Presidency is gathered into Article II, as supplemented and altered by the veto procedure in Article I, and by Amendments XII, XX, and XXII. All these amendments, and most of Article II, concern the eligibility, choice, and tenure of the President. As we turn to the enumerated presidential powers, what is astonishing is their total inadequacy to support the office as we know it today.

Of these powers, two are without substance, although not without effect in establishing a conception of the office. "[H]e may require the Opinion, in writing, of the principal Officer in each of the executive Departments, upon any Subject relating to the Duties of their respective Offices . . ." "He shall from time to time give to the Congress Information of the State of the Union, and recommend to their Consideration such Measures as he shall judge necessary and expedient. . . ."

Two other powers are of peripheral significance and evidently cannot importantly define a great office: ". . . [H]e shall have the power to grant Reprieves and Pardons for Offenses against the United States, except in Cases of Impeachment." ". . . [H]e may on extraordinary Occasions, convene both Houses, or either of them, and in Case of Disagreement between them, with Respect to the Time of Adjournment, he may adjourn them to such Time as he shall think proper. . . ."

This leaves five enumerated powers: (1) The "commander-in-chief" power; (2) The treaty power, together with the power to receive envoys; (3) The veto power; (4) The appointing power; (5) The power (or duty) to take care that the laws be "faithfully executed."

The military power is qualified by the powers of Congress to declare war, to make rules for the land and naval forces, to maintain the army and navy, to provide for calling out the militia, and others, as well as by Congress' power over appropriations. A "commandership-in-chief" subject to such control might without remark have become symbolic only.

The power of the President over foreign relations has called forth admiring rhetoric, and is remarkably great, as it now exists. But its textual ground is narrow. The treaty power, its chief stated content, is to be exercised with the "advice," as well as the "consent," of the Senate, and is placed at the mercy of one-third plus one of that body. The power to "receive" envoys need be no more than formal; on its face, indeed, this provision imports no power at all, but rather a mandated duty. The power to appoint envoys will be dealt with below, under the appointing power in general; for now it should be noted that it stands in the Senate's hand.

Congress (besides being vested, as we have seen above, with the powers of war and peace) is given control over duties, foreign commercial intercourse, naturalization, the valuation of foreign coin, and "offenses against the Law of Nations." Congress, and not the President, has the power to "make all Laws which shall be necessary and proper for carrying into Execution the foregoing Powers. . . ." If we had only text, and no history, the inference would be nearly irresistible that our foreign affairs were to be managed by Congress, with the President, under close congressional supervision, doing a few things that must for the sake of efficiency be done by the Executive.

The veto power may shortly be dealt with—or, rather, it might have been shortly dealt with if Congress and the people had thought it well to dispose of it, for a convention might easily have arisen (and for that matter might still arise) that vetoes were always to be voted down by the requisite two-thirds. Such a convention would have increased the power of Congress and hence, on the average and in the long run, of every member of Congress.

The fate of the appointing power, next on the above list, shows that a presidential power may be reduced by congressional convention to less than its seeming extent. In fact, the members of the Senate, and even of the House, exert an enormous prior influence on appointments. In part, this influence takes the firmly institutionalized form of "senatorial courtesy"; appointments within a state are made in obedience to the wishes of those senators from that state who are of the President's own party; appointments not so made are commonly not confirmed.[1] A less channelized set of influences emanates from highly placed members of either House. Nominally "presidential" appointments in fact are resultants of manifold pressures, from and through Congress.

None of this is in the text. But it shows what can be done with the text. Probably such illustration by history is needless. An appointing power which is at the mercy of the Senate, which appoints to offices created and paid by Congress, with such duties as Congress may give them, is a power that can be made just as ineffectually formal as Congress wants to make it.

Finally, the President "shall take Care that the Laws be faithfully executed. . . ." The "laws" are mostly acts of Congress. But even more important is the fact that Congress has to provide the means of execution.

One other important and permanently controversial provision is not included in the list above. Article II begins: "The executive Power shall be vested in a President of the United States of America. . . ." This provision can be construed in two general ways—either as giving a name to the officer who is to wield the powers soon to be enumerated, and as establishing that there shall be one such officer instead of more than one, or as conferring on the President a general power—the "executive" power—in addition to those to be enumerated. The second construction opens the way to an indeterminate number of specific definitions of the "executive" power; its acceptance must significantly affect the conception of the Presidency. There is no conclusive reason for choosing between these modes. The tenability of the second mode was in the hands of tradition and history. If Congress had made the veto power a nullity, had taken foreign affairs broadly under its own control, had dictated appointments to a much greater extent than has been the case, and had run the government through its own committees, the argument that the President enjoyed wide "executive power" would scarcely have had any substance.

The upshot is that under the Constitution, as it came from the Convention, the Presidency stood within the shadow of Congress. Without straining a single provision in the text, Congress might have made the President into a symbolic chef d'état. His enumerated powers are those commonly enjoyed by persons in that position.

It cannot be our business here to sound the reasons—in political dynamics, in social psychology—for the development that has actually taken place. The legal articulations of this development are simple in outline (although exceedingly complex in detail). First, Congress, instead of reducing the Executive to a formal status, has by its own laws steadily added to his power; most of the legally warrantable powers of the Presidency today come from statutes. Secondly, the office itself has been able to claim and make good large powers not easily found in the text.

An important step in the development of the Presidency was the early institution of the party system, controlling election both to the Presidency and to Congress. The natural corollary was the present conception of the

[1] See Louis Brownlow, *The President and the Presidency* (Chicago: Public Administration Service, 1949), pp. 76–77.

President as head of his party, which is normally the party in command of Congress. It may be conjectured, too, that a rigidly bicameral structure of Congress inhibited the development of the most likely alternative to presidential primacy—parliamentary government on the British model. The British House of Lords could be disposed of, both by the material threat of the creation of new peers, and by the moral argument that it had no claim, as an hereditary chamber, to decisive voice in a democracy. The Senate enjoys protection against change in its constituency and numbers even by constitutional amendment,[2] and it not only is an elective body (and has always been that in an indirect sense, even before the Seventeenth Amendment) but has a claim, as the guardian of equality among the states, that sounds deep in our political tradition. Of our two Houses, neither has a unique claim to be the base of parliamentary government; that may have facilitated the devolution of leadership on the most conspicuously available office outside either.[3]

THE EXECUTIVE DEPARTMENT; "DELEGATION"

As stated above, probably the most important presidential powers, and certainly the most numerous, are those the President gets by delegation from Congress. It may be, then, that the most significant judicial legitimation of presidential power has been the Court's wide approval of this process of delegation—to the President or to officers controlled by him. The standard objection is soberly clothed in a maxim—"*Delegata potestas delegari non potest*"—a delegated power may not itself be delegated. Congress is "delegated" by the people. The maxim stands formally unrejected, if one regards it as not forbidding congressional empowerment of the Executive to act according to "standards" laid down by Congress; in that case, one can say, Congress is still "legislating," and the Executive is merely following the legislative "standards." The catch is that these standards may (with Court approval) be so broad as to amount to an invitation to make policy. Delegations (to the President and to subordinates controlled by him) have been vague and sweeping. An important case was Field v. Clark (1892),[4] upholding a delegation to the President of power to suspend importation of articles after ascertaining certain facts; dispensing and altering powers under the tariff have been continually broadened.[5] U.S. v. Grimaud (1911)[6] sustained a delegation (to the Secretary of Agriculture) of a regulatory power, legislative in all but name, over forest reserves.

Abundantly delegating, Congress has sometimes sought to retain some control. The President has, for example, been given power to promulgate extensive "reorganization plans," affecting the whole Executive Department, but these powers have been made subject, in the laws authorizing them, to congressional veto. The Lend-Lease Act of World War II provided on its face

[2]Article V.
[3]It is believed that this suggestion is somewhere made by Professor Corwin.
[4]143 U.S. 649.
[5]See, e.g., Hampton v. U.S., 276 U.S. 394 (1928).
[6]220 U.S. 506.

that it could be brought to an end by concurrent resolution of both Houses (not subject to presidential veto). This provision has been attacked as an unconstitutional encroachment on the President's veto power, but there seems to be no reason why Congress, which can provide that the expiration of legislation is to be contingent on events, may not make expiration contingent on the event of positive expression of congressional disapproval.[7]

"Delegation" from Congress largely defines the President's powers; "sub-delegation" by him enables him to use his powers. One man could not so much as supervise all the decisions he is empowered to make. The Court has early[8] and late[9] given broad approval to the necessary process of presidential sub-delegation.

REMOVAL

The necessity of wide delegation of legislative powers—of running the affairs of government through executive and administrative agencies—has led to the multiplication of such agencies, and to a permanent war between Congress and the President for their control. They are "executive" in that they carry out policy, but they are for the same reason Congress' agents for exerting its powers. Who is to run them?

The most significant judicial interpretation here is in the removal cases. The Constitution provides for appointing officers, but not for their removal. In the First Congress (1789), the decision was taken to concede to the President power to remove certain department heads, but in the nature of the case it is hard to be sure whether this was a recognition of presidential right, or Congress' relinquishment of its own claim.[10] In 1867 Congress (distrusting President Johnson) made the members of his Cabinet unremovable. At his impeachment trial his violation of this act was defended principally on the ground that he had a right to test its constitutionality.[11] The removal question was given extended consideration by the Court in Myers v. U.S. (1926).[12] Myers, a postmaster, held office under an act of Congress which made him removable only with Senate concurrence. He was removed by the President, without such concurrence, and his estate sued for his salary. The Supreme Court denied his claim, painting with a broad brush:

> . . . The ordinary duties of officers prescribed by statute come under the general administrative control of the President by virtue of the general grant to him of the executive power, and he may properly supervise and guide their construction of the statutes under which they act in order to secure that unitary and uniform execution of the laws

---

[7]J. Malcolm Smith and Cornelius P. Cotter, *Powers of the President during Crises* (Washington, D.C.: Public Affairs Press, 1960), pp. 106–109. See Edward S. Corwin, *The President: Office and Powers* (New York: New York University Press, 1957), pp. 129–130.

[8]Williams v. U.S., 1 How. (42 U.S.) 290 (1843).

[9]Ludecke v. Watkins, 335 U.S. 160 (1948).

[10]See the opinion in the Myers case, *infra*, note 12.

[11]Wilfred E. Binkley, *President and Congress* (New York: Alfred A. Knopf, Inc., 1947), pp. 139–144.

[12]272 U.S. 52.

which Article II of the Constitution evidently contemplated in vesting general executive power in the President alone. . . . Finding such officers to be negligent and inefficient, the President should have the power to remove them.

But Humphrey's Executor v. U.S. (1935)[13] so limited this doctrine as to leave the President with much less removal power than the Myers case seemed to bestow. A member of the Federal Trade Commission, during a term fixed by statute at 7 years, was removed by President Roosevelt on the ground that ". . . your mind and my mind [do not] go along together . . . ," the best of reasons for removing a political subordinate. But the Court confined the Myers doctrine to an office that was "merely one of the units of the executive department. . . ." It was denied application to members of independent commissions set up by Congress to further its own policies.

Since removal by Congress is not practically adaptable as a means of procuring unity in policy formation, the result of this decision is that the members of powerful boards and commissions cannot be brought into line with the publicly stated current policy of any elected official or body. True, a President sooner or later gets a chance to make some appointments of his own, but (aside from the time-lag involved) this is no guarantee of cooperation; people change when they get tenure. It would seem that enough lag potential is built into a bureaucracy, especially a civil-service bureaucracy, without making some of its principal officers immune from executive control.

The Humphrey decision was handed down in 1935, when the Court's hostility to Roosevelt's program was at its highest. It has since been limited. In 1941 the Court refused to review a holding that it did not apply to removal of a director of the Tennessee Valley Authority, which ". . . exercises predominantly an administrative or executive function. . . ."[14] But in Weiner v. U.S. (1958)[15] a member of the War Claims Commission was held irremovable, since that commission exercised functions of an "intrinsic judicial character." This view of the War Claims Commission is doubtless right, but it could be wished that the Humphrey rule could be limited to such agencies.

In the execution of laws, and hence in the fulfillment of the executive function, there is always some discretion, some factor of policy; it is symmetrical with our governmental scheme to place those boards that are charged with the duty to take care that particular laws are faithfully executed (and that is, for example, the relation of the Interstate Commerce Commission to the Interstate Commerce Act and later statutes) firmly under the control of the elected officer who stands under that duty with regard to all laws.

"EXECUTIVE PRIVILEGE"

One problem in interdepartmental relations has never come to issue in court. Congress, through its committees, has a right to investigate the operations

---

[13]295 U.S. 602.
[14]Morgan v. T.V.A., 115 Federal Reporter, 2d Series 990 (Sixth Circuit Court of Appeals 1940), *certiorari denied*, 312 U.S. 701 (1941).
[15]357 U.S. 349.

of government. The President, on the other hand, is responsible for the work of his own official family. Discharging that responsibility may in his judgment require secrecy. Time after time, congressional committees have sought access to matters held secret by order of the President, who has asserted an "executive privilege" against disclosure. The good sense of the antagonists has always produced compromise. It may be that the presence of the Court, as potential umpire, has facilitated this compromise. Either party may fear that statement of rules of law will threaten its position; claims of immunity or of disclosure could then be made matters of legal right. However that may be, conflict in the judicial forum has always been forestalled.

WHO MAKES NATIONAL POLICY?

The most interesting problems about relations between the branches of government concern their respective powers to form policy and make law. There is no doubt that Congress is the chief law-making and policy-forming branch. There is no doubt that the President has some purely constitutional policy-forming power—his veto, his appointments, his function as negotiator of treaties, his continuing control of foreign affairs, his role as commander-in-chief, all give him this authority, as they are traditionally understood. But how wide are the President's purely constitutional powers? When Congress has passed no legislation on the subject concerned? Or when Congress has spoken adversely to the President's position? These questions are raised in the great modern case of Youngstown Sheet and Tube v. Sawyer (1952).[16]

A general steel strike, threatened for January 1, 1952, was postponed by the union pending an investigation by the Federal Wage Stabilization Board. The union accepted the board's recommendation, but management rejected it, and a new strike call was set for April 9. The Korean War was in progress.

President Truman might at this point have gone into court under the Taft-Hartley Act and applied for an injunction imposing an 80-day cooling-off period. Perhaps because the union had already voluntarily postponed the strike for longer than 80 days, and had accepted the proposal of the only responsible public agency that had considered the dispute, Mr. Truman chose not to follow this course, which would be of benefit only to management, and ordered "seizure" of the plants, doubtless intending to negotiate a settlement with the union. The steel companies sued to enjoin the carrying out of this order.

Uncontestedly, Truman was not acting under any statute; his power to "seize" must come, if it existed, from his purely constitutional position as President. His counsel invoked the "stewardship" theory of his office, earlier stated by Theodore Roosevelt.[17] As the holder of "executive power," as commander-in-chief, and as the officer responsible for the execution of the laws, he was (it was argued) authorized to take such steps as were necessary to guard vital national interests.

[16]343 U.S. 579.   [17]P. 5 of Brownlow, *op. cit. supra*, note 1.

Mr. Justice Black, in an opinion designated as that "of the Court," rejected this theory of the Presidency. The command power to seize property for the supply of troops existed, said he, only in a theater of war. The "executive" power was no more than the power to carry out congressional policy as expressed in acts of Congress. The powers to take property for public use, and to regulate labor relations, were vested in Congress, and hence not in the President. No utterance could go much further in confining the Presidency within the narrow bounds of an almost ministerial conception of the office.

But 4 of the 5 Justices who concurred with Black in result (Frankfurter, Jackson, Clark, and Burton) stated their reasons in separate opinions that cannot be reconciled with Black's views, while three (Vinson, Reed, and Minton) dissented even from the result. The concurrers (except Douglas) found decisive the negative implication of the Taft-Hartley Act. They thought, in effect, that Congress had impliedly forbidden the action Truman had taken, and they judged the presidential power in that light. The issue to them was, "Had the President power to do this in the teeth of Congress?" and not "Would the President have had this power from the Constitution, if Congress had not expressed its views?" It must be left to conjecture why they joined an "opinion of the Court" with which they did not agree.

With respect, Justice Black's view is unhistoric and unworkable. If there had been no congressional utterance on the matter, and if none could be procured, it is quite plain that this strike had nevertheless to be avoided in some fashion. There were many precedents, in and out of the Court, for the President's acting on his own regarding matters on which Congress also might act; the dissenting opinion cites most of these.

The case actually reaffirmed[18] that when Congress has directed, or implied, that a certain action is not to be taken, the President's power to take that action is to be narrowly regarded. The President doubtless has some power even of this irreducible kind; Congress could not order him to appoint only experienced judges to the Supreme Court, to command that a battle be fought in a certain way, or to veto no bills. But if Congress determines to stake the national safety on one mode only of dealing with crippling national strikes in wartime, such a decision might be held to take away the President's power as well as his responsibility. The troublesome question in the Youngstown decision was whether the Supreme Court should have picked up such an intention from mere negative implication; Congress had never actually said, "No seizure." It may be reasonable to require that congressional negative on presidential acts affecting the security of the nation be definite and express.

Perhaps by design, the net effect of the Youngstown case has been to leave open the entire question of executive power as a supplement to congressional power.

PRESIDENT AND COURT

The incidence of anything recognizable as constitutional "law" on relations between Congress and the President is only partial. The role of the President

[18]Cf. Little v. Barreme, 2 Cranch (6 U.S.) 170 (1804).

in recommending legislation fluctuates with forces that have no legal savor. The veto is uncontrolled. With "senatorial courtesy" the Court has nothing to do.

At some points, however, judicial umpiring is significant. The removal power is in process of judicial definition. The Youngstown case, however blurred it is in some respects, gives legal status to an idea of the Presidency somewhere between the "messenger-boy" theory and the theory of wide power exercisable in conflict with Congress' express will. The positions taken on the "executive privilege" of non-disclosure have probably been softened by the knowledge that the Court will decide if issue is ever firmly joined. The tradition of constitutional legality plays some part, moreover, in discussion of some presidential actions that can never come to the Court. A significant though far from all-pervasive part is played by law, spoken by the Court, in defining the relations between executive and legislative powers.

CHAPTER FIVE

FOREIGN RELATIONS AND WAR

THE WAYS OF PEACE

The President, the Senate, and the States. The constitutional law of our foreign relations involves Congress, the President, and the states. Although the states may seem excluded in principle, the breadth and effect of the exclusion are fighting matters. In foreign affairs the United States acts as a unit. The states may not make treaties, or do other things (such as waging war or keeping armies) which entail international complications (Article I, §10). Nevertheless, the development of the unitary foreign relations power of the United States has raised problems of much the same sort as those that are unfolded in other developments of national power—problems of state autonomy, as well as of federal interdepartmental relations.

In Article II, the President is given power, "by and with the Advice and Consent of the Senate, to make Treaties, provided two thirds of the Senators present concur . . ." and to "receive Ambassadors and other public Ministers; . . ." The appointment of our diplomatic representatives falls within his general appointing power. Article VI stipulates that ". . . all Treaties made or which shall be made under the Authority of the United States, shall be the supreme Law of the Land. . . ."

As is pointed out in the discussion of the Presidency (Chapter 4), it is not obvious that the quoted language gives the President warrant to claim by grant that primacy in the conduct of foreign affairs which prescription now gives him. It was originally proposed in the Convention to vest the treaty-making power wholly in the Senate; the provision as it stands might be read as a not crucially different form of this, conceding to the Executive the initiative, but keeping the function tightly under Senate control. When the Constitution came into being, the Senate was to have 26 members—few enough to sit around a large table—and the concept of its collectively "advising" the President on treaty matters was not absurd. This procedure was tested; Washington visited the Senate chamber to discuss a proposed Indian treaty. Strain on protocol, and uncertainty about primacy, made the occasion embarrassing; the practice since has consisted in formally independent presidential negotiation of treaties, with subsequent submission of these to the Senate.[1]

The role of the Senate remains one of vast constitutional importance. Here is disconformity between myth and prose, between reputed and possessed power. The President and his diplomatic subordinates go about as accredited representatives of the United States; we ourselves see them as that. Yet they cannot commit the nation to a treaty if 34 senators, who could represent something like 15 per cent of the people, withhold concurrence.

This provision is of questionable wisdom. The Senate is constituted to protect state and regional interests, the separatist and divisive interests in a federal union. Yet in the case of treaties, where the nation is most to be envisaged as a unit (with sectional interests correspondingly muted), the Senate is given a veto, strongly accentuated by the two-thirds rule. The results have been dramatic; many think them unhappy. The annexation of Texas had to be accomplished by by-passing the Senate.[2] The United States was kept out of the League of Nations by Senate veto. It is a mistake, moreover, to think of the Senate's role as confined to ratification or rejection of treaties. Its ultimate power in this regard gives to it, and especially to its Foreign Relations Committee, a considerable, although unformalized, say in the conduct of foreign policy.

This senatorial influence is not unconstitutional or even extra-constitutional. To "advise," as well as to "consent," is the Senate's role, and the unwisdom of this, if unwisdom it be, stems from the Constitution and not from usurpation by the Senate. But the place of the Senate in treaty-making has (as we shall later see) given impetus to exploration of alternative routes to international arrangements.

The Treaty as Law. We will have nothing to say here about the treaty as an obligation in international law. Instead we will turn to the consequences of treaties' having the force of law within the United States. The passage quoted from Article VI, on p. 20, suggests several questions: May a treaty become "law" of its own force, without being implemented by a federal statute? May a treaty be "law" with respect to any subject, or can it be "law" only within those fields over which the federal government is given authority elsewhere in the Constitution? May the "law" of a treaty validly infringe an express constitutional prohibition, such as the free-speech guarantee? What if a treaty contravenes a prior act of Congress? What if a subsequent act of Congress contravenes a treaty?

Several of these questions are answered in Hauenstein v. Lynham

[1]See Edward S. Corwin and Louis W. Koenig, *The Presidency Today* (New York: New York University Press, 1956), p. 49.
[2]Justin H. Smith, *The Annexation of Texas* (New York: Baker & Taylor, 1911), pp. 258–280.

(1880).³ A Swiss citizen died in Virginia without having made a will. He owned Richmond real estate. His heirs, who would inherit in the absence of a will, were also Swiss citizens. Under Virginia law, aliens were incapable of inheriting real estate; the state brought proceedings for forfeiture. The Swiss heirs petitioned to have the property sold and the proceeds paid to them, claiming this right under a treaty. The Court read the treaty as applying to the situation. What, then, was its effect? The Court said:

> That the laws of the State, irrespective of the treaty, would put the fund into her coffers, is no objection to the right or the remedy claimed. . . .
>
> [T]he Constitution, laws and treaties of the United States are as much a part of the law of every State as its own local laws and Constitution. This is a fundamental principle in our system of complex national polity. . . .

First, the treaty was regarded as "self-executing"—its provisions had the force of law without any further congressional action. Whether a treaty is self-executing is a question of its interpretation. Some treaties are clearly meant to state rules of law binding within the signatory nations. Other treaties do no more than obligate the signatory nations to enact laws later, in implementation of the treaty. If these laws are not enacted, then the treaty is violated, but no implementing law exists within the nation that has so failed in its obligation, and the courts of that nation will not enforce the treaty as law. As in every matter of interpretation, there are borderline cases. The important thing is that a treaty *may* be valid as law, without further legislation, if that is what is wanted and intended. National law may be made, through treaty, by President and Senate, without concurrence of the House of Representatives.

Secondly, the provisions of the Hauenstein treaty, having been construed as "self-executing," were held to prevail over state law. This seems the necessary consequence of the supremacy clause, quoted on page 20.

Thirdly, in Hauenstein v. Lynham, the Court was unworried by the question whether the subject covered by the treaty provision—the legal consequences of real estate's descending to a foreign national—was one over which the federal government would have had power to act in the *absence* of a treaty—under, say, Article I, Section 8. The point has to be put in this guarded way, for clear decisions on this issue are hard to come by. Treaties always deal with matters of international interest, and the federal government is broadly empowered, outside the treaty power, to deal with such matters. In the Hauenstein case, for example, it is arguable that Congress might permissibly conclude that foreign commerce would be fostered by relieving alien residents from the drastic consequences of forfeiture, and so pass a valid law to that general effect, without a treaty. The most one can say, therefore, is that the Court appears unconcerned with the question.

This last point came to issue, in language at least, in Missouri v. Holland (1920).⁴ Some years before the decision, Congress had passed a law regulating

³100 U.S. 483.   ⁴252 U.S. 416.

the killing of birds that migrated from one state to another. Several lower federal courts had held this statute to be outside the power of Congress. A treaty with Great Britain was then made, pursuant to which Congress again passed a law dealing with the subject. Missouri sued to enjoin enforcement. The opinion puts the treaty power on an independent footing:

> It is said that a treaty cannot be valid if it infringes the Constitution, that there are limits, therefore, to the treaty-making power, and that one such limit is that what an act of Congress could not do unaided, in derogation of the powers reserved to the States, a treaty cannot do.
>
> [This] cannot be accepted as a test of the treaty power. . . . We do not mean to imply that there are no qualifications to the treaty-making power; but they must be ascertained in a different way. It is obvious that there may be matters of the sharpest exigency for the national well being that an act of Congress could not deal with but that a treaty followed by such an act could, and it is not lightly to be assumed that, in matters requiring national action, "a power which must belong to and somewhere reside in every civilized government" is not to be found. . . .

It has always been assumed that the treaty power, like all the other powers of the federal government, is subject to the express prohibitions contained in the Bill of Rights and elsewhere in the Constitution—that a treaty, for example, could not validly make illegal, in the United States, the criticism of General Franco, or provide that crimes committed here against Swiss residents were to be tried without a jury. In Reid v. Covert (1957)[5] an "executive agreement" with Britain (which the Court seemed to view as for the purpose tantamount to a treaty; see *infra*, pp. 68 ff.) permitted trial by United States military courts of civilian dependents accompanying our military personnel in Britain. The wife of a serviceman had been tried for murder by an American court-martial in England; her *habeas corpus* petition raised the claim that military trial violated her constitutional rights. Said the Court:

> . . . It would be manifestly contrary to the objectives of those who created the Constitution, as well as those who were responsible for the Bill of Rights—let alone alien to our entire constitutional history and tradition—to construe Article VI as permitting the United States to exercise power under an international agreement without observing constitutional prohibitions.

What is the position when a federal statute transgresses an earlier treaty? In the Chinese Exclusion Case (1889),[6] a treaty with China had extended to Chinese subjects working in this country the privileges of "the most favored nation"; implementing this treaty Congress had enacted that Chinese laborers in the country on the date of the treaty might procure a certificate of identity, which would entitle them to re-enter if they left temporarily. While the holder of such a certificate was absent from the country, Congress repealed the law, substituting a stringent provision against re-entry, and voiding the certificates. The Court denied re-entry, holding that Congress might (even under

[5]354 U.S. 1.   [6]130 U.S. 581.

circumstances which made the act not only perfidious but cruel) abrogate the treaty at will. A treaty, considered as law, is then on the same footing as any other law; it may be repealed by a later law. (This repudiation cannot affect the *international* obligation; it was still open to the Chinese government, as a government, to protest the violation of the treaty.)

The Executive Agreement. From earliest times international agreements other than treaties have been entered into by the President, acting either alone or in pursuance to some power delegated to him by Congress. Questions have arisen about the permissible scope and effect of these "agreements." The essence of the matter is that they bypass the two-thirds rule in the Senate; even when they are authorized or implemented by Congress they need pass the Senate by only a simple majority. Let us survey some of the issues.

Congress is extensively empowered to deal with subjects which concern foreign relations. There are foreign aspects to any subject, but it is enough to enumerate foreign commerce, war, foreign coin, maritime offenses, and the post office. To make an agreement concerning a given subject is often the most practical way of dealing with that subject. The power to establish a postal system cannot be exercised, in regard to foreign mail, without making agreements with foreign countries. "Commerce with foreign Nations" is often most effectively "regulated" by making agreements. Agreement with a foreign nation, on one of the subjects Congress is empowered to deal with, would therefore seem to be one of the "necessary and proper" ways of Congress' acting upon that subject. In practice, direct action by Congress would be unwieldy. Congress, acting within its Article I, Section 8, powers, has sometimes delegated to the President, as its representative and subject to such standards as it sets, the power to negotiate such agreements. The 1934 Reciprocal Tariff Act[7] is an example. In it Congress gave power to the President to negotiate with foreign countries for reciprocal reductions in import duties. Congress has the power to fix the amounts of import duties—both under its taxing power and under its power to regulate foreign commerce. Exercising this power, it had, within stated limits, authorized the President to proclaim modification of existing tariffs (see p. 58). Since Congress might lower these rates one by one, or in a new schedule each year, any objection to the thing's being done in the only practical way must be the narrow one of "improper delegation"—but Congress has wide powers of delegation, especially to the President. This power of delegation has been held to be broadest in foreign affairs.[8]

The Constitution may then be read to warrant Congress' authorizing the President, as its representative, to make agreements with foreign nations on all the subjects placed under Congress' hand by the Constitution. Nor need chronological order make much difference. If the President has negotiated an advantageous agreement dealing with patents, and Congress chooses thereafter to adopt it and enact it into law, may not that be a "necessary and proper" means of "securing . . . to Inventors . . . the Right to their . . . Discoveries . . ."?

---

[7] 48 Statutes at Large 943.   [8] U.S. v. Curtiss-Wright Export Corp., 299 U.S. 304 (1936).

On this basis alone, the power of Congress, acting through the President, to give assent to international agreements, would be in theory narrower than the treaty power, for Missouri v. Holland (like many other cases) suggests that the treaty power is not limited to subjects otherwise under federal authority, while agreements made under the theory just sketched must deal with subjects confided to Congress by the Constitution. But few subjects that are likely to be dealt with in treaties would at this time be held outside Congress' power under Article I, Section 8. If such a subject is found, then presumably it could be dealt with only by treaty.

A similar line of thought can support a considerable power in the President to make pure "executive agreements" on his own. The President is "Commander-in-Chief" of the armed forces. It seems plausible that part of a "commander's" power is the power to make agreements with respect to his command. In 1940, for example, President Roosevelt made an agreement with Britain, providing for the lease to us of certain bases, in exchange for our giving Britain 50 destroyers.[9] The acquisition of bases is a recognized function of command; there seems no objection to the use of the device of "agreement" to this end. Similarly, the President (being authorized to send ambassadors) is surely authorized to agree to do so.[10]

Insofar as it rests on this theory—that power to handle a matter includes power to handle it by agreement—our concept of the scope of presidential power to make independent executive agreements, must follow the contours of our concept of presidential power as a whole—a subject elsewhere discussed (*supra*, pp. 55–60). Here, it should be remarked that the concept of the Presidency as the locus of an extensive power over international affairs is firmly fixed in constitutional tradition.

Against this theoretical background may be set some modern cases. In United States v. Belmont (1937)[11] President Roosevelt had (in connection with recognition of the Soviet Union) accepted the "Litvinoff Assignment" of Russian assets in the United States, including a deposit in a New York bank, standing to the credit of a pre-Revolution Russian corporation, and "nationalized" by Soviet decree in 1918. The United States, as assignee of the confiscating government, sued the banker's executor, who contended that (since the deposit was in New York) the public policy of that state, which opposed confiscation, must prevail. The Court disfavored this claim. The agreement, it said, was not a "treaty" so as to require Senate ratification, but was a "treaty" so as to be the "supreme Law of the Land." As such, it overrode the policy of New York, for, "Plainly, the external powers of the United States are to be exercised without regard to state laws or policies." This view was strongly reaffirmed in United States v. Pink (1942).[12]

If one added these holdings to the doctrine of Missouri v. Holland, a disquieting sum was possible. The Pink and Belmont decisions might be read as saying that any agreements at all might be "annexed" to the presidential act of recognition, or to others of his official acts, and that these

---

[9]Edward S. Corwin, *The President: Office and Powers* (New York: New York University Press, 1957), p. 238.
[10]See Craig Mathews, "The Constitutional Power of the President to Conclude International Agreements," 64 *Yale Law Journal* 345 (1955).
[11]301 U.S. 324.   [12]315 U.S. 203.

"agreements" then took on the status of treaties, though not requiring any form of ratification, and so became the "law of the land," overriding state law. But if they were tantamount to "treaties," then, under Missouri v. Holland, they need not even concern federal subjects. The President, as a part of "recognizing" Saudi Arabia, might agree that polygamy be henceforth lawful, perhaps even obligatory, in the United States. About so ran the fears, which were heightened by a 1950 state court decision. The United Nations Charter, ratified as a treaty by the Senate, contained some general language about immunity from racial discrimination, and a lower California court held this treaty "self-executing" (see the discussion of Hauenstein v. Lynham, *supra*) and judged that it invalidated the state law that prohibited land ownership by Japanese.[13] The Supreme Court of California, although affirming the decision, repudiated this ground, resting the matter on the Fourteenth Amendment.[14] But the fears remained.

The result was a series of proposals (the "Bricker Amendment" and its later substitutes) for limiting the treaty and "executive agreement" powers.[15] All failed of passage; the fears that engendered them may now be partly quieted by the decision in Reid v. Covert, mentioned earlier, for at least it is now clear that the Bill of Rights limits the treaty power and its functional equivalents. The only other recent case-law has also tended to quiet apprehension. In Capps v. U.S. (1953)[16] a federal Court of Appeals held an executive agreement void because it contradicted a prior act of Congress.

THE WAYS OF WAR

Congress is given the power to "declare war." This power has not worked to place much actual decision-making authority in Congress' hands. War may begin by our being attacked; we are then at war, and Congress can only take note. The President has been left by Congress in broad charge of foreign relations; his actions may come so close to committing the country that Congress can do nothing but take the final step.

President Lincoln, early in 1861, set up a blockade of southern ports; its legality depended on the existence of a state of war. In the Prize Cases (1863)[17] the Court (5–4) upheld the President's power to act in the face of actual hostilities. Hostilities in Vietnam have been conducted without declaration of war by Congress; it was contended that prior treaty obligations, and the "Tonkin Bay" resolution of 1964, made such declaration unnecessary. The Supreme Court denied certiorari in the case of a soldier suing to enjoin military authorities from sending him to Vietnam; this left the underlying constitutional questions unsettled. Justices Stewart and Douglas dissented,

---

[13]Fujii v. State, 217 Pacific Reporter, 2d Series, 481.

[14]38 Calif. Reports, 2d Series, 718.

[15]Arthur Sutherland, "Restricting the Treaty Power," 65 *Harvard Law Review* 1305 (1952); "The Bricker Amendment, Executive Agreements, and Imported Potatoes," 67 *id.* 281 (1953).

[16]204 Federal Reporter, 2d Series 655 (Fourth Circuit Court of Appeals, 1953). The case was affirmed in the Supreme Court on another ground, 348 U.S. 296 (1955).

[17]2 Black (67 U.S.) 635.

with opinions, from the certiorari denial, insisting that the Court should hear argument and decide the issues.[18]

The existence of war has never been held to suspend the Constitution, but the powers of the President and Congress are measured in wartime on a scale that takes account of the fact that war exists. Some powers (like that of blockade) come into existence only as a result of war; the United States may, for example, seize and vest in itself the property of enemy nationals.[19] Other powers have been held greatly expanded. Federal rent control was first put forward as a war measure in World War I;[20] a general national prohibition law, prior to the Eighteenth Amendment, was sustained on the ground that, by conserving materials and men, it increased efficiency for purposes connected with war.[21]

Congress may reach deep into areas of state authority for war purposes. In Stewart v. Kahn (1871)[22] it was held, for example, that Congress had power to suspend the running of state statutes of limitation during periods when access to state courts was blocked by war. Various federal statutes have given relief to soldiers and sailors from the normal operation of state laws; the validity of these has been assumed.[23]

The "war power," both in itself and as a handy name for the expansion of Congress' other powers, does not end when the shooting ends. The prohibition statute mentioned earlier was passed after the armistice, but the Court held that the problems of demobilization kept alive enough of the war power to sustain the statute. Federal rent control was held valid during the period following World War II.[24]

The most striking effect of the existence of war, in modern times, is the enormous growth in presidential power. Delegation of power from Congress—always his chief source of authority—put the President in a near-dictatorial status during World War II. The Lend-Lease Act of 1940 is an impressive example. The President was empowered (even before the country was legally at war) to procure any "defense articles" and dispose of them on such terms as he saw fit to "any country whose defense the President deems vital to the defense of the United States." Allocation of material was authorized, price controls set up, plant seizures provided for—all within the discretionary control of the President. Where these and like dispensations were questioned in court, they were always sustained.[25]

Military government of enemy territory is a normal incident of war. At times the military establishment (which means, ultimately, the President) has sought to substitute military for civilian rule in territory normally subject to our Constitution. Ex parte Milligan (1866)[26] is a landmark, now considerably weathered. During the Civil War, active southern sympathizers, even in loyal areas remote from battle, were sometimes arrested by the military and

[18]Mora v. McNamara, 88 Supreme Court Reporter 282 (1967).
[19]Silesian-Amer. Corp. v. Clark, 332 U.S. 469 (1947).
[20]Block v. Hirsh, 256 U.S. 135 (1921).
[21]Hamilton v. Ky. Distilleries Co., 251 U.S. 146 (1919).
[22]11 Wall. (78 U.S.) 493.
[23]See Boone v. Lightner, 319 U.S. 561 (1943).
[24]Woods v. Miller, 333 U.S. 138 (1948).
[25]E.g., Yakus v. U.S., 321 U.S. 414 (1944).
[26]4 Wall. (71 U.S.) 2.

tried by "commissions" of army officers. Milligan had been so dealt with in Indiana. The Court (from the safe ground of 1866) held this procedure unlawful, since civil courts were open in Indiana. The opinion seemed to say that trial of civilians by military tribunals was unlawful unless in areas where the civil authority was practically out of business.

The military is not easily discouraged. In Hawaii after Pearl Harbor the governor of the Territory proclaimed "martial law," closed civil courts, and turned governmental powers over to the local commanding general. Convictions for embezzlement and assault were procured against civilians in military courts. The Court reversed, but left the constitutional question open, basing the judgment on construction of the Hawaiian Organic Act.[27]

A number of recent decisions have invalidated expansion of court-martial jurisdiction beyond persons actually in the military. In Toth v. Quarles (1955)[28] the Court released an airman who had been honorably discharged and then arrested and flown back to Korea to be court-martialed for an offense he was alleged to have committed while in service. Civilian dependents and employees (it has recently been settled) cannot be court-martialed for offenses committed overseas.[29] In Wilson v. Girard (1957),[30] on the other hand, it was held that an American soldier serving in Japan might be turned over to the Japanese for trial on a charge of having killed a Japanese civilian.

Perhaps the most drastic exertion of military power over civilians which our history contains is the one upheld in Korematsu v. U.S. (1944).[31] A military "exclusion order," issued by a general commanding on the West Coast, ordered all persons of Japanese ancestry, aliens or not, out of a large section of the country. Connected provisions ordered them not merely to leave, but to do so via "assembly points," whence a large number of them were sent to "relocation centers"—concentration camps. In the Korematsu case the Court was asked to reverse a conviction, obtained in a civilian federal court, on the charge of remaining within the area after the order became effective. Korematsu was a citizen of the United States; his own loyalty was not questioned. The Court sustained the conviction.

As Mr. Justice Jackson, dissenting, pointed out, it would have been possible for the Court to refuse actively to interfere with this military program of racial evacuation, without affirmatively lending the aid of the civilian courts to send people to jail. It should be noted that the immediate "order" which Korematsu violated was not that of Congress or of the President. An act of Congress made it generally criminal to violate any such order, and the President, as commander-in-chief, was ultimately responsible for the order; but the judgment that the particular order was necessary was uttered by a local general. It would seem reasonable to require, at least before the civilian courts of the United States are to be used to penalize citizens for refusing to be herded into concentration camps, either that Congress specifically prohibit their continued residence in their homes, or that the President himself take the solemn responsibility before history of publicly sponsoring the concrete individual judgment that military necessity requires their removal and deten-

[27]Duncan v. Kahanamoku, 327 U.S. 304 (1946).   [28]350 U.S. 11.
[29]Reid v. Covert, 354 U.S. 1 (1957). See *supra*, p. 67.   [30]354 U.S. 524.   [31]323 U.S. 214.

tion. That judgment was military, but not exclusively so; it was one as to which that union of civilian and military control, realized in the Presidency, was of profoundest relevance.

Ex parte Endo,[32] decided the same day, somewhat softened the rigor of the Korematsu decision, but its facts showed how little weight the military power, and the people in charge of the whole disastrous concentration-camp program, were minded to give to the claims of citizens of Japanese ancestry. Miss Endo, a former civil-service employee in California, was of *conceded* loyalty to the United States. The War Relocation Authority nevertheless insisted it had a right to hold her in the Tule Lake "Relocation Center"; her release, it was said, might stir up trouble, the bureaucrat's *bête noire*. That there were some limits to the Court's tolerance was shown by the decision to grant her *habeas corpus*. This action was not rested, however, on constitutional grounds, but on a holding that the legislation and executive orders involved did not authorize holding concededly loyal persons.

[32]323 U.S. 283.

CHAPTER SIX

INDIVIDUAL RIGHTS AGAINST GOVERNMENT

GENERAL VIEW

The Texts and Their Interconnections. The law with which we have so far dealt is in strict terms "constitutional," having to do with the reach and distribution of powers. We now turn to a new kind of constitutional law— that establishing limitations on power.

The original Constitution placed prohibitions on the national government. Most are in Article I, Section 9; a few are scattered elsewhere, like the Article III prohibition of prosecutions for "treason" not amounting to an overt act. These safeguards, although minimal, are of high theoretical importance; they establish that it never has been a warranted tenet of our system that the people's representatives for the time being are to do whatever they think wise and good. However it may view the morality or policy of the matter, Congress is not to vote a bill of attainder, or to impose a tax on exports. This concept of binding limitation on the transient majority's will and judgment is coeval with the Republic; it is as authentic as any political idea we have.

The Constitution also contains limitations on the states, mostly in Article I, Section 10. These do not have the same theoretical bearing as those that run against the national government; even without them it could not be thought that state legislative authority is limitless. Expressing national requirements in regard to state action, they do not differ, in their effect on state law, from acts of Congress. But their occurrence in the original Constitution is interesting from another point of view. Some of them exclude the states from areas of material national concern, such as foreign relations. Others, like the prohibition on state import taxes, aim at commercial unity. But some point in another direction. They embody elementary conceptions of justice: "No State shall . . . pass any Bill of Attainder. . . ." These provisions establish that it is a congenital part of our constitutional theory that the states are to be limited in the interest not only of tangible national goals but also of national ideals of justice.

The subsequent textual history of "constitutional limitations" consists in addition by amendment. The first addition was the so-called Bill of Rights— the first ten amendments, ratified by 1791. The second was of the Thirteenth, Fourteenth, and Fifteenth Amendments, ratified during Reconstruction. Except for the unproblematic Nineteenth Amendment, giving women the vote, this completes the canon.

Some of these prohibitions run against the national power, some against the states, and some against both. Questions as to where each prohibition falls have not always been easy to resolve. The earliest case in this regard concerned the Bill of Rights, the first ten amendments. Amendment I is on its face directed against the federal power only: "Congress shall make no law. . . ." Others are expressed generally, in the passive voice: "Excessive bail shall not be required. . . ." Someone was sure to contend that these amendments, so expressed, applied not only to federal but to state activity. The test came in 1833.[1] A city damaged a wharf; the owner contended this amounted to "taking" his property. He claimed that the Fifth Amendment (". . . nor shall private property be taken for public use, without just compensation.") was a declaration of "principles which regulate the legislation of the States. . . ." A unanimous Court denied that the Bill of Rights applied to the states.

Up to the Civil War, then, federal constitutional protection against state action had to be drawn out of the original Constitution, unsupplemented by the Bill of Rights; this protection was quite limited. The Fourteenth Amendment, in 1868, effected a sweeping change:

> §1. All persons born or naturalized in the United States, and subject to the jurisdiction thereof, are citizens of the United States and of the State wherein they reside. No State shall make or enforce any law which shall abridge the privileges or immunities of citizens of the United States; nor shall any State deprive any person of life, liberty, or property, without due process of law; nor deny to any person within its jurisdiction the equal protection of the laws.

> .   .   .   .   .

> §5. The Congress shall have power to enforce, by appropriate legislation, the provisions of this article.

These words threw up a vast federal shield against the states. Their grammatical form was the same as that of the older protection against state "ex post facto" laws and bills of attainder. But the new language, instead of being sparely technical, was very broad. The Court's problem since has been to give it meaning.

One help to achieving such specificity, where it can work, is the discernment that general language may properly be construed to incorporate more specific language found elsewhere. It was inevitable, then, that the

---

[1] Barron v. Baltimore, 7 Pet. (32 U.S.) 243.

contention would be made that the Fourteenth Amendment "incorporated" the Bill of Rights.

The Court has in terms rejected the theory of total "incorporation." In Walker v. Sauvinet (1876)[2] a litigant in a state court demanded trial by jury in a civil case. He would have had this right in a federal court, by the Seventh Amendment. The Supreme Court made short work of his contention that the Fourteenth Amendment "incorporated" this provision:

> By art. 7 of the amendments, it is provided that "in suits at common law, where the value in controversy shall exceed twenty dollars, the right of trial by jury shall be preserved." This . . . relates only to trials in the courts of the United States. : . . A trial by jury . . . in the State courts is not . . . a privilege or immunity of national citizenship, which the States are forbidden by the Fourteenth Amendment to abridge.

This position was restated again and again, regarding a number of specific Bill of Rights guarantees.

Meanwhile a counter-current had developed. First, "due process of law" obviously required basic fairness in the procedures by which law was administered. A man had no federal right to a jury in state court,[3] but he did have a right to an impartial jury if a jury were used.[4] This was not because the Fourteenth Amendment "incorporated" the Sixth Amendment right to an "impartial jury," but because the "due process of law" of the Fourteenth Amendment itself called for impartiality in the triers of fact. Since many of the procedural guarantees of the Bill of Rights themselves rested on common conceptions of fairness, it was inevitable that the process of construing the Fourteenth Amendment would eventuate in the imposition on the states of something resembling the Bill of Rights provisions.

In recent years, this process has gone so far that little is left of the "non-incorporation" doctrine. Older cases[5] holding that the Fifth Amendment federal privilege against self-incrimination is not binding on the states, by virtue of the Fourteenth Amendment, have been overruled.[6] A state prosecutor or judge may not even comment on a defendant's refusal to testify.[7] The Fifth Amendment right to be confronted by the witnesses against one is now held guaranteed by the Fourteenth.[8] The Sixth Amendment right to a speedy trial has been similarly treated.[9] On the whole, very little remains of the "non-incorporation" doctrine, as a practical matter, in the field of criminal "due process."

Meanwhile, virtual "incorporation" was proceeding by another route. Content had to be given to the "liberty" guaranteed by the Fourteenth

---

[2]92 U.S. 90.
[3]Maxwell v. Dow, 176 U.S. 581 (1900).
[4]See Strauder v. W. Va., 100 U.S. 303 (1880).
[5]Twining v. N.J., 211 U.S. 78 (1908); Adamson v. Calif., 332 U.S. 46 (1947).
[6]Malloy v. Hogan, 378 U.S. 1 (1964).
[7]Griffin v. Calif., 380 U.S. 609 (1965).
[8]Pointer v. Texas, 380 U.S. 400 (1965).
[9]Klopfer v. N.C., 386 U.S. 213 (1967).

Amendment. From Allgeyer v. Louisiana (1897)[10] a spacious view of "liberty" began to be insisted on:

> The liberty mentioned in that amendment means not only the right of the citizen to be free from the mere physical restraint of his person, as by incarceration, but the term is deemed to embrace the right of the citizen to be free in the enjoyment of all his faculties; to be free to use them in all lawful ways; to live and work where he will; to earn his livelihood by any lawful calling; to pursue any livelihood or avocation. . . .

At first, this wide range of definition chiefly shielded business rights. But in the 1920's the Court extended the federal shield over non-economic "liberties." In Meyer v. Nebraska (1923)[11] the Court held unconstitutional a statute forbidding school-teaching in any language but English: "His right thus to teach and the rights of parents to engage him so to instruct their children, we think, are within the liberty of the [14th] Amendment." And in Pierce v. Society of Sisters (1925)[12] the Court struck down a state law requiring attendance at public schools only, speaking of the "liberty of parents and guardians to direct the upbringing and education of children under their control. . . ."

After this, the Bill of Rights "incorporation" issue had to arise in a new form. If the "liberty" of the Fourteenth Amendment includes the right to raise children as one wishes, must it not include the "freedom of speech" protected by the First Amendment against federal invasion? In 1925, in Gitlow v. New York,[13] the Supreme Court said it did, and since that time "free-speech" problems have been treated as much the same, whether a state or the nation was the government "abridging" the freedom. The same pattern of reasoning has brought into the Fourteenth Amendment the guarantees against religious establishment and compulsion.[14]

"Incorporation" of the Bill of Rights into the Fourteenth Amendment has not, then, taken place formally. But the virtual equivalent has occurred. On the side of procedure, the Fourteenth Amendment requirement of "fairness" often comes down to something like a specific Bill of Rights requirement. On the side of substance, the First Amendment has as good as been incorporated (although not without problems, as we shall see). The working line has sometimes been seen as the one drawn by Mr. Justice Cardozo, speaking for the Court in Palko v. Connecticut (1937):[15]

> There emerges . . . a rationalizing principle. . . . The right to trial by jury and the immunity from prosecution except as the result of an indictment may have value and importance. Even so, they are not of the very essence of a scheme of ordered liberty. . . .
> We reach a different plane of social and moral values when we pass to the privileges and immunities that have been taken over from the earlier articles of the federal bill of rights and brought within the Four-

---

[10]165 U.S. 578.   [11]262 U.S. 390.   [12]268 U.S. 510.   [13]268 U.S. 652.
[14]See McCollum v. Board of Education, 333 U.S. 203 (1948).   [15]302 U.S. 319.

teenth Amendment by a process of absorption. . . . If the Fourteenth Amendment has absorbed them, the process of absorption has had its source in the belief that neither liberty nor justice would exist if they were sacrificed. . . . This is true, for illustration, of freedom of thought, and speech. . . . Fundamental too in the concept of due process, and so in that of liberty, is the thought that condemnation shall be rendered only after trial. . . . The hearing, moreover, must be a real one, not a sham or a pretense. . . . For that reason, ignorant defendants in a capital case were held to have been condemned unlawfully when in truth, though not in form, they were refused the aid of counsel. . . . The decision did not turn upon the fact that the benefit of counsel would have been guaranteed to the defendants by the provisions of the Sixth Amendment if they had been prosecuted in a federal court. The decision turned upon the fact that in the particular situation laid before us in the evidence the benefit of counsel was essential to the substance of a hearing.

On procedural matters, this position is intelligible, giving rise to questions only of detail. When substantive rights (such as free speech) are brought into the Fourteenth Amendment as "liberties," a difficulty remains, though it is not much discussed. For the Fourteenth Amendment does not (how could it?) forbid "deprivation of liberty" in all cases, but only where there is deprivation "without due process of law." Strictly speaking, it is not enough to invalidate a state law that it "abridge the freedom of speech"; it must do so "without due process of law."

The Weighing of Interests. "Due process of law," at a minimum, means "procedural regularity and fairness." It is also settled that "due process" is infringed when a law is in its substance wholly "arbitrary," when there is no arguably rational connection between the measure taken and some permissible state objective. If this criterion were applied, Fourteenth Amendment protection in free-speech cases (for example) would disappear. There is always room for a rational (though not necessarily a correct) view that the suppressive law will serve some good purpose. The application of the "due process" clause to state enactments suppressing speech requires, then, the articulation of a stricter requirement of justification for the suppressive law than the mere absence of irrationality.

The field in which this problem must be (and has not clearly been) faced can be widened by recurring to Pierce v. Society of Sisters. The "liberty" there protected was that of sending one's children to the school of one's choice. In the general discourse of "due process," as sketched above, the Pierce judgment would have to rest on a finding that no reasonable legislator could decide that valid state objectives, such as unity of feeling and community of experience among all citizens, would be served by requiring all children to attend public school, or that the state's interest in having a well-educated citizenry would most efficiently be served by the state's seeing to the matter itself. To bring this issue out is to resolve it; a rational man surely might conclude—though not all rational men need do so—that social values were to be served by requiring a common education, and that these values were to be preferred to those served by parental independence. As to some "liberties," "due process" must require something more than arguable rationality, if the Pierce decision is to stand.

At this point the Court is called on for a value judgment, for a decision as to where these weighty interests are located. Many factors must go into the making of this judgment. In regard to the matters covered by the First Amendment (freedom of speech, religion, assembly), the Court has the aid of a political judgment, made at the adoption of the amendment, that these subjects were of such high importance that even Congress was to be restrained from dealing with them freely, if at all. That judgment, even if the First Amendment is not "incorporated" into the Fourteenth, is surely of aid in ranking the First Amendment interests in our historically warranted hierarchy of values, for the purpose of ascertaining the content of Fourteenth Amendment "due process."

During a part of the Court's history, now a generation past, extravagant protection was extended to business immunity from state regulation. This was done principally through the use of the Fourteenth Amendment "due process" clause. The Court said that its duty was to nullify only those state regulations for which no reasoned justification could be proffered; actually, it sometimes invalidated state laws which regulated business in ways which were easily susceptible to rational justification, but which the judges thought unwise. By a process more familiar than logical, some later justices, commanding at times a majority, have insisted on overcompensating for this by excessive deference to legislative judgment, even in areas where the Constitution itself takes that dim view of legislative judgment which is implied by its putting the legislature under express restraints. Even the verbally unqualified prohibitions of the First Amendment are spoken of as though that amendment were another "due process" clause, forbidding only that congressional action which has no arguably rational basis. This is judicial fiat merely—just as distortive as was the conversion of the "due process" clause into an invitation to the Court to act as a revisory council on the prudential questions raised by economic regulations. It is an impoverished reasoning which can draw no distinction for judicial function between the "due process" inference invalidating "arbitrary" legislation and the command of the First Amendment.

For different reasons, the Fifth and Fourteenth Amendment command of "due process," in its *procedural* aspect, ought to be enforced by the Court broadly and without embarrassment. That command is that a fair procedure characterize the acts of authority. Conformity of procedure to the best that can now reasonably be looked for is a matter judges are particularly qualified to supervise.

Outside the specially protected fields (free speech, jury trial, search and seizure, right to counsel, and so forth) and the field of procedural due process, there remains that area, of great delicacy, where the Court is asked to give a preferred ranking to a substantive interest, to place it above legislative interference. Pierce v. Society of Sisters, as we have seen, was such a case. It is interesting that the Pierce Court was unanimous; Holmes and Brandeis, at the time in full revolt against their brethren's excessive use of the due-process clause, joined an opinion which said:

> [W]e think it entirely plain that the Act of 1922 unreasonably interferes with the liberty of parents and guardians to direct the upbringing and education of children under their control. As often heretofore pointed out, rights guaranteed by the Constitution may not be abridged by legislation which has no reasonable relation to some purpose within the competency of the State. The fundamental theory of liberty upon which all governments in this Union repose excludes any general power of the State to standardize its children by forcing them to accept instruction from public teachers only. The child is not the mere creature of the State; those who nurture him and direct his destiny have the right, coupled with the high duty, to recognize and prepare him for additional obligations.

Herein is acceptance, by the two Justices who of all others were most sensitive to the requirements of deference to legislative judgment, of the proposition that some interests can confidently be identified, even under the due-process clause, which are too precious for the legislature to tamper with. They must have seen the recognition of such interests as a part of the business of judging. The interest of parents in educating their children is not the only such interest. This part of the judge's role presents difficult problems, but is it really hard to say that there is more historically and culturally warranted value in the claim to give one's children a religious education than there is in the claim to underpay one's employees?

(This judicial ranking of interests is sometimes spoken of as entailing a choice between the protection of "property rights" and of "personal rights." No such blunt issue is tendered. "Freedom of the press" is a freedom, principally, in the use of property; even the "free speech" case may involve the use of a sound truck or other chattels. Fairness in criminal procedure protects against fines and confiscations as well as against imprisonment. The case outlawing the racial restrictive covenant[16] confirmed a Negro in the most ancient of property rights, that of living in his house. The ranking is rather among different uses of both person and property.)

Unembarrassed judicial activism is justified beyond doubt in those fields where substantive rights are protected by name in the Constitution, and where the question of fair procedure, a lawyer's professional specialty, is before the Court. But unless Pierce v. Society of Sisters is wrong (and who today is prepared to say it is?), the Court ought also to be ready to protect some vital interests against hostile legislation, even though they have no such clear textual claim nor such clear credentials as indispensable components of the political process.

The most recent assumption by the Court of this most rarely exercised of its functions was in Griswold v. Connecticut,[17] the last in the series of Connecticut birth-control cases.[18] Relying on Pierce v. Society of Sisters and

[16]Shelley v. Kraemer, 334 U.S. 1 (1948).   [17]381 U.S. 479 (1965).
[18]See *supra*, pp. 6 and 9.

Meyers v. Nebraska, the Court held that the state might not intrude upon the intimacies of the marital relation by prohibiting the use of contraceptives.

Rights Arising from Political Relations. Up to now we have considered constitutional limitations as rooting in particular textual provisions ("freedom of speech," "due process of law"). There is another possible source of such protections, as yet not much developed in decision. Like congressional and presidential powers, limitations may sometimes arise by implication from the nature and structure of our polity. The slight development till now of this branch of the law may be due to a preference in our juristic style for the "interpretation" of indubitably authentic commands, rather than the discernment of implications. But this stylistic preference may change.

Crandall v. Nevada (1868)[19] is an excellent illustration. Nevada imposed a "capitation tax of one dollar upon every person leaving the State . . . by any . . . vehicle . . . transporting passengers for hire, . . ." The Court, invalidating the tax, reasoned directly from the unitary character of the nation to the correlative rights of citizens:

> The people of these United States constitute one nation. They have a government in which all of them are deeply interested. This government has necessarily a capital established by law, where its principal operations are conducted. . . . The government, also, has its offices of secondary importance in all other parts of the country. On the seacoasts and on the rivers it has its ports of entry. . . . In all these it demands the services of its citizens, and is entitled to bring them to those points from all quarters of the nation, and no power can exist in a State to obstruct this right that would not enable it to defeat the purposes for which the government was established. . . .
>
> But if the government has these rights on her own account, the citizen also has correlative rights. . . . [A]nd this right is in its nature independent of the will of any State over whose soil he must pass in the exercise of it.

With the possible reservation that the dollar tax may have been *de minimis*, insufficient to be thought a substantial barrier, this is surely sound reasoning. It rests on no single text, but on the nature of our national system.

The case was decided before the adoption of the Fourteenth Amendment, with its clause providing: "No State shall . . . abridge the privileges and immunities of citizens of the United States. . . ." Since that clause was adopted, discussion of relational rights of persons, arising from their being members of the national polity, has centered about its language. The Court very early held that it protected only those "privileges and immunities" which flowed from the relationship of the citizen to the national government; as has often been pointed out, this robbed the clause of additive meaning, for it is to be presumed that the states were already disabled from abridging "privileges and immunities" of that sort.

[19]6 Wall. (73 U.S.) 35.

The Court has as yet made no use of this clause, even as restricted. This reluctance may be rooted in the fact that it protects only "citizens," while the "due process" and "equal protection" clauses protect "persons," including aliens. But unwillingness to exclude non-citizens from minimal constitutional protection need not generate a fear of recourse to the Crandall v. Nevada concept. If the Fourteenth Amendment "privileges and immunities" clause added nothing, surely it subtracted nothing. And the national government has profound reciprocal relations, capable of generating rights, not only with citizens but also with aliens. Crandall v. Nevada may yet become a fountainhead case.[20]

Very often, the question whether protection for a right or immunity is to be worked out on "due process" or "equal protection" grounds, rather than through the relational implications of membership in the national polity, is practically without importance; the same protection can be extended either way. But it is sometimes possible to construct a more satisfying rationale on grounds of relational implication. Where such an inference is sound, it is the most satisfying of all, for it rests inherently in the nature of our politics. Many interesting instances of the judicial deduction of relational rights from the fact of membership in the national polity (and other relations therewith) are collected in Brewer v. Hoxie School District (1956).[21] (The Eighth Circuit U.S. Court of Appeals enjoined interference with a school board's performance of its duty to give an unsegregated education to children.) Another example will be offered when we take up the problem of federal protection against state infringement of freedom of speech.

A Look Forward. The rest of this chapter will deal with three special problems in the law of constitutional limitations. They are selected only as illustrations; even to mention all important problems is not feasible. The selection is of three major contemporary areas of developing constitutional protection: (1) freedom of speech on political subjects; (2) protection from racial discrimination; (3) the right to fair procedure in the administration of law.

As to each of these, an attempt will be made to sketch a development, omitting many details. The reader should ask, in each case, "What is the national interest underlying the set of guarantees being examined?"

One general observation is applicable to every recurrence of this question. It may sometimes be assumed, in an age of tangibles, that a national interest, to be valid, must be a tangible, even a utilitarian interest. National interests of this sort exist and must be served. But the assumption that they are the only national interests worth talking about is one of those "hidden major premises" that fade in the light. There may be national interests of a wholly moral kind—in minimal justice, in the eradication of cruel and ignorant discrimination, in respect for intellectual freedom—to which practical factors are adventitious. Beyond everything tangible, our basic constitutional guarantees express national interests of this order.

[20]Edwards v. Calif., *supra*, Chapter 2, note 69, might have been decided on Crandall v. Nevada grounds.
[21]238 Federal Reporter, 2d Series, 91.

FREEDOM OF EXPRESSION

The Texts. The First Amendment says that Congress "shall make no law . . . abridging the freedom of speech, or of the press; or the right of the people peaceably to assemble, and to petition the Government for a redress of grievances." No distinction of importance has been drawn between the "speech" and "press" freedoms. The Fourteenth Amendment provides that "no State shall . . . deprive any person of . . . liberty . . . without due process of law; . . ." It has been held that the freedoms of speech and of the press are among the Fourteenth Amendment "liberties."[22] No clear distinction has been drawn between state infringement and federal infringement of either of these rights. As we have seen (p. 78), this "incorporation" creates a problem; but since it is a problem that has not been adequately faced in the decisions, it will be best to give a combined account of certain decisions on state and federal laws, and then to consider the special difficulties that arise with state laws.

If we except the notorious Alien and Sedition Laws of 1798, which have by common consent been hung in the closet, the First Amendment, until well in the twentieth century, had (like a happy people) no history. Through two wars[23] vigorously opposed at home, and even when a whole region was in rebellion, with loyal sections full of wordy rebel sympathizers, Congress passed "no law . . . abridging the freedom of speech, or of the press. . . ." Practically speaking, the history of the suppression of political speech in the United States, by the federal civil power, begins with the Espionage Act of 1917. (Problems concerning the suppression of non-political utterance, by both state and nation, have existed much longer. "Obscenity" and "sacrilege" are important categories. Summarily, the Court has held "obscenity" unprotected, but has so defined that term as to include only prurient matter without "redeeming social importance."[24] The suppression of "sacrilege" raises questions, so far not settled, concerning the First Amendment guarantee against any law "respecting" the establishment of religion.)

"Seditious" Utterance. The most commonly assigned reason for suppressing utterance is that it is "seditious"—that it threatens the safety of the state. (This is also the most dangerous reason, because it inevitably conduces to the suppression of serious political protest.) On its face, the First Amendment would not appear to admit of the suppression of such utterance. Few people, however, would read this guarantee as a genuine absolute. To do so raises great difficulties; protection of "speech" which would immunize a speaker who exhorts a mob to proceed at once to burn city hall is something not likely to be accepted in our culture. The master-problem has been whether plain imminence of serious evil, without opportunity for further discussion or other measures, is to be the only excuse for suppressing utter-

---

[22]See *supra*, p. 77.
[23]Protest was wide and sustained throughout the War of 1812 and the Mexican War.
[24]Roth v. U.S., 354 U.S. 476 (1957).

ances, or whether they are to be suppressed because of a "tendency" to produce threats to public safety at some later time, with more or less debatable causal nexus between the speech and the evil. The first is about all the protection free speech is likely to get. The second amounts to no protection at all, and nullifies the First Amendment: the most suppressive laws in history have needed no other justification than the "bad tendency" of the suppressed speech.

In practice, then, "free speech" must admit exceptions from *necessity*. The fighting occurs when the "necessity" invoked is not exigent and demonstrable, but only inferential or metaphoric.

The early landmark is Schenck v. U.S. (1919).[25] The Supreme Court has not yet fully digested Mr. Justice Holmes' opinion, for the Court that affirmed the conviction. The charge was distributing (in wartime) a leaflet expressing opposition to the draft. Said Holmes: "The question in every case is whether the words used are used in such circumstances and are of such a nature as to create a clear and present danger that they will bring about the substantive evils that Congress has a right to prevent."

Here the famous "clear and present danger" test began its life. That test is an attempt to solve the problem stated in the first paragraph of this section. If "clear" means really "clear," not "inferred from current dogma" or "assumed to be clear because Congress has acted," and if "present" means "present," and if "danger" means a peril which firm-minded men, dedicated to freedom of speech, could regard as serious enough to justify its suppression, then the test gives free speech something like all it can hope for, if not all it might get in a world of steadier faith. The more pestilential obstructions to freedom of opinion must always have something to apologize for, as long as even lip service is given to this test.

Soon after Schenck, in Abrams v. U.S. (1919),[26] Holmes (with Brandeis) dissented from affirmance of conviction, contending that either present danger of immediate evil or an intent to bring it about must exist before utterance could be punished, and that neither of these had been shown (as surely they had not). If he had stopped there, the distinction from Schenck would have been clear; "intent" to encompass a forbidden result was believed by Holmes to be proved in Schenck and unproved in Abrams. He did not stop, but uttered words that seem as inconsistent with the Schenck as with the Abrams conviction, words which in fifty years have lost none of their beauty, or of their feel of authenticity, or of their power to sadden one who peruses subsequent decisions:

> But when men have realized that time has upset many fighting faiths, they may come to believe even more than they believe the very foundations of their own conduct that the ultimate good desired is better reached by free trade in ideas—that the best test of truth is the power of the thought to get itself accepted in the competition of the market, and that truth is the only ground upon which their wishes safely can be carried out. That at any rate is the theory of our Constitution. It is an experiment, as all life is an experiment. . . . While that experiment is

[25]249 U.S. 47.   [26]250 U.S. 616.

part of our system I think that we should be eternally vigilant against attempts to check the expression of opinions that we loathe and believe to be fraught with death, unless they so imminently threaten immediate interference with the lawful and pressing purposes of the law that an immediate check is required to save the country. . . . Only the emergency that makes it immediately dangerous to leave the correction of evil counsels to time warrants making any exception to the sweeping command, "Congress shall make.no law . . . abridging the freedom of speech."

In this passage, clearly, "intent" is no substitute for real danger, and that danger is not of a vague open class of "evils that Congress has a right to prevent" (such as smoking in Pullman cars on interstate trains), but an evident and imminent danger of national ruin, something *even more* than a belief that an opinion is "fraught with death." In the Schenck opinion and in this last passage two Holmeses spoke; the time since has not sufficed for final decision as to which of them is to be followed.

In Gitlow v. New York (1925),[27] the Supreme Court sat on the case of a "criminal anarchist," convicted by New York of teaching "the duty, necessity and propriety of overthrowing . . . government . . . by force, violence and unlawful means. . . ." (The application of the First Amendment to state law was first approved in this case; this point will be specially treated later.) Gitlow had issued a manifesto, in the turgid rhetoric of the *genre*, calling for "proletarian struggle" and mass strikes. There was no showing of any kind of danger. (The danger the case actually illustrated was the danger in sedition statutes; the New York law seemed on its face to apply only to definite advocacy of violent revolution, but the finding that Gitlow was guilty of this had to rest on inferences and "reading between the lines.") The Court majority applied the standards of "reasonableness," and of deference to legislative judgment, and affirmed.

Holmes and Brandeis once more dissented. And in Whitney v. California (1927)[28] they gave (Brandeis writing) the most careful definition to date of "clear and present danger": ". . . [N]o danger flowing from speech can be deemed clear and present, unless the incidence of the evil apprehended is so imminent that it may befall before there is opportunity for full discussion." A "present" danger, according to this view, must be "present"—and the mode of statement places this requirement of "presence" in the context from which freedom of speech gets its value—namely, the assumed rationality of the public, and its capacity to resist bad counsel when time is available for good.

After the Whitney case, the Court majority seemed to have said that "freedom of speech" was not infringed if the class of utterance to which the defendant's words belonged might conceivably be judged to have a tendency to produce untoward consequences. But this position failed to produce general satisfaction. It clashed with the Schenck words, "clear and present danger." It reduced freedom of utterance to nothing; no legislative body could be expected to enact any measure which could not pass this test. The

[27]*Supra*, note 13.   [28]274 U.S. 357.

words of Holmes and Brandeis, in the Abrams and Whitney cases, had a quality which kept alive their ideas.

In Stromberg v. California (1931)[29] something of a turn was taken. Conviction was under a state law which penalized the display of a red flag "as a sign, symbol, or emblem of opposition to organized government. . . . " The Supreme Court reversed, harmonizing previous cases by noting that the statute did not distinguish between peaceable and violent "opposition to organized government." But this was, to say the least, a limitation not inherent in the principles followed in the Gitlow case. Wide diffusion of sentiments of opposition to government is surely something a "reasonable" legislature might wish to prevent; it might "reasonably" be concluded that such a climate of opinion is favorable to revolution. The foreclosing of these "reasonable" conclusions meant some stiffening of the Gitlow standard, and put a little substance into the guarantee of free expression.

De Jonge v. Oregon (1937)[30] reversed a conviction for having presided over a public meeting of the Communist party, an organization which the jury had found to advocate criminal syndicalism and sabotage. The Court held that, since the very meeting was not shown to have been other than peaceable, the defendant could not be convicted simply because the party was elsewhere advocating things that might under the Gitlow and Whitney decisions be penalized. But surely a "reasonable" legislator might conclude that the holding of meetings by such groups increased their chances of success, even when the particular meeting did not concern the unlawful part of their aims. Again, then, the Court was insisting on something more than mere "reasonableness" as a defining characteristic of the statute that could leap the First Amendment bar.

In following years there developed a feeling in many quarters, and on the part of some Justices, that freedom of speech, although not "absolute," enjoyed something like a "preferred position"—that the mere possibility that legislation abridging it might avert some evil was not enough to justify its abridgment. By 1949 Mr. Justice Reed could refer to this "preferred position" as to a thing well-known.[31]

By 1950, then, something like the following principles might be taken to have standing:

1. The right to freedom of expression on political topics was not "absolute," but was to yield to some considerations of public safety.
2. On the other hand, no statute suppressing utterance could survive on a mere showing that a reasonable man could think it might do some good, or avert some evil.
3. The "clear and present danger" test had some claim to being the most widely accepted accommodation.

Against this background came Dennis v. U.S. (1951).[32] The defendants, Communists, were indicted under the Smith Act of 1940 for (1) conspiring to form a party which was to teach and advocate the overthrow of the govern-

[29]283 U.S. 359.   [30]299 U.S. 353.   [31]Kovacs v. Cooper, 336 U.S. 77.
[32]341 U.S. 494.

ment by violence, and for (2) conspiring to advocate the duty and necessity of such overthrow. Their chief contention was that the statute, as applied to them, could not pass the "clear and present danger" test. Conviction was affirmed.

The writer of the main Dennis opinion, Mr. Chief Justice Vinson, first interprets the Court's past acceptance of this test in a most restrictive way. But he goes on:

> Although no case subsequent to Whitney and Gitlow has expressly overruled the majority opinions in those cases, there is little doubt that subsequent opinions have inclined toward the Holmes-Brandeis rationale. . . .
>
> In this case we are squarely presented with the application of the 'clear and present danger' test, and must decide what that phrase imports. . . .
>
> Chief Judge Learned Hand, writing for the majority below, interpreted the phrase as follows: "In each case [courts] must ask whether the gravity of the 'evil,' discounted by its improbability, justifies such invasion of free speech as is necessary to avoid the danger." 183 F. 2d at 212. We adopt this statement of the rule.

Two problems are seen—the seriousness of the threatened evil, and the reality or closeness of the threat.

Attempted rebellion is a serious evil, although it may be doomed to failure. The troublesome thing about the Dennis opinion is its dealing with the question of the actual imminence of such attempt. The defendants were not even charged with "advocating," but with conspiring to advocate, this attempt; "presence," predicated of such a "danger," loses all meaning. It was found that they intended to advocate making the attempt whenever in their view it should become feasible, and the Court, in affirming the conviction, seems to treat as irrelevant any consideration concerning the probable time at which this judgment would be made, or even the probability of its ever being made.

This may (or may not) be wisdom, but it is not, as the Vinson opinion makes it out to be, an "application" of the "clear and present danger test." That test is reduced to the estate of Voltaire's Holy Roman Empire: "Neither Holy, nor Roman, nor an Empire."

Later cases have somewhat softened Dennis. Yates v. U.S. (1957)[33] gave effect to a distinction, foreshadowed in Dennis, between "incitement to action" and "advocacy of ideas," holding the latter uncovered by the Smith Act. It is hard to give form to this distinction; the idea that government ought to be overthrown is surely an incitement of sorts to overthrow it. Still, Yates may have reintroduced some of the "clear and present" danger test *sub rosa*, for the incitement *power* of an utterance may depend on its relation to a state of things in which action is likely.

The Yates case exemplifies a process by which the Court has often protected free speech. Instead of resting on constitutional grounds, it con-

[33]354 U.S. 298.

strued the statute narrowly. This is an orthodox and long-sanctioned procedure, where constitutional values come into play. The strict construction of statutes which might, if broadly construed, offend constitutional guarantees, spares the Court from deciding the ultimate constitutional question. And when a statute comes even close to violating the Constitution, it is reasonable to ask that Congress take full political responsibility for the infringement of individual rights.

Such protection as the Court has given to free speech, as against *federal* power, has been worked out in this way. In reviewing dismissals of government employees for security reasons,[34] in dealing with the use of Congress' investigative power to harass individuals for political opinions,[35] and elsewhere,[36] the Court has frequently insisted on hewing the line precisely to the wording of the statute or other authority, or even on reading into it such qualifications as were needed to save it from constitutional doubt.

Two cases decided on the same day (Scales v. U.S.[37] and Noto v. U.S.[38]) bracketed a compromise position. Both cases came up from convictions of Communists under the clause of the Smith Act penalizing knowing membership in any society advocating the overthrow of the government by violence. This "membership" clause was upheld in the abstract, but very strict proof was demanded of all the elements of the crime, including the defendants' knowledge of the unlawful purpose of the party. Scales was affirmed (5–4) and Noto reversed, on the ground that the illegal aims of the party had been satisfactorily shown by evidence in the first case, but not in the second.

Until quite lately, then, protection of speech on political topics from *federal* infringement has worked out about as follows: (1) The Court has never had to deal with an act of Congress which attempted to penalize political speech except on grounds of ultimate national security. As to such statutes, it has given only lip service to the "clear and present danger" test and to all other tests that would put teeth in the First Amendment; (2) But the Court has required that Congress make its intent to penalize political speech quite clear, and that the government strictly prove its case.

This does not measure up to the faith of Holmes's Abrams dissent (p. 84, *supra*), or to Jefferson's First Inaugural: "If there be any among us who would wish to dissolve this Union, or to change its Republican form, let them stand undisturbed as monuments of the safety with which error of opinion may be tolerated, where reason is left free to combat it." Those for whom the invisible palladium of America was the thought in these words cannot rest satisfied with the Dennis decision and its sequel. Two recent cases, Aptheker v. Sec'y of State[39] and U.S. v. Robel[40] may presage

[34] E.g., Vitarelli v. Seaton, 359 U.S. 535 (1959); Cole v. Young, 351 U.S. 536 (1956).
[35] E.g., Watkins v. U.S., 354 U.S. 178 (1957).
[36] E.g., Kent and Briehl v. Dulles, 357 U.S. 116 (1958). A generally phrased statute and executive order were construed not to give the Secretary of State power to withhold passports on grounds of political affiliation.
[37] 367 U.S. 203 (1961).
[38] 367 U.S. 290 (1961).
[39] 378 U.S. 500 (1964).
[40] 389 U.S. 258 (1967).

a new departure. In each, Congress had annexed a disability (ineligibility for a passport in Aptheker and for "defense industry" employment in Robel) to mere membership in the Communist party, without proof of knowledge of the party's unlawful aims. The Court struck down both statutes on First Amendment grounds, declining to rewrite them so as to save their constitutionality. Also, the 1965 case of Lamont v. Postmaster General[41] struck down a statute requiring the destruction of certain mail determined to be "political propaganda." It is too early to predict where these cases may lead.

The States and Free Speech. The states have sought to suppress speech for miscellaneous reasons of public order, as well as for protecting the safety of society. Supreme Court precedents on such regulations show little consistency, partly because the majorities on one side or the other have tended to be narrow, and partly because the interests protected (and the forms of suppression) vary so widely as to make abstraction difficult.

Terminiello v. Chicago (1949)[42] and Feiner v. New York (1951)[43] make an interesting pair. Terminiello was convicted of disorderly conduct, on evidence which showed that, under conditions which made rioting extremely likely, he delivered a speech of which a fair sample, from the report of the case, seems the contrast drawn between "Christians" and "scum." Bricks, stink-bombs, and bottles were thrown. The Court, by a 5–4 vote, reversed. Said Mr. Justice Douglas, ". . . a function of free speech under our system of government is to invite dispute." In the Feiner case, 2 years later, a conviction of disorderly conduct was affirmed. Feiner had made a provocative speech (containing crudely derogatory remarks about public officials) and had refused to stop talking when police ordered him to do so, a measure they judged necessary for keeping order. There was some evidence of possible impending trouble, but nothing near the Terminiello situation. The opinion of the Court rests on recognition of the state's interest in preventing riot. It may be technically possible to harmonize these two cases. But the lay reader of the opinions would hardly believe they were decided by the same Court.

Beauharnais v. Illinois (1952)[44] further illustrates the Court's divisions on "public-order" state laws infringing free speech. Beauharnais published an anti-Negro leaflet, and was convicted under a statute forbidding any publication ". . . which . . . portrays depravity, criminality, unchastity, or lack of virtue of a class of citizens . . ." or exposes them to "contempt, derision, or obloquy. . . ." Again, by a 5–4 vote, the Court affirmed. Mr. Justice Frankfurter's opinion gets around the "clear and present danger" test by finding an analogy between the forbidden publications and the "libeling" of a single individual. The dissents scattered in views.

The tenor and tendency of the suppressed opinion have not always been crucial in the state cases; sometimes factors of public convenience and comfort enter. In Saia v. New York (1948)[45] the Court (5–4) reversed a conviction under a statute prohibiting the use of sound-trucks without a permit. The following year, in Kovacs v. Cooper (1949),[46] again 5–4, the Court

---

[41]381 U.S. 301.   [42]337 U.S. 1.   [43]340 U.S. 315.   [44]343 U.S. 250.
[45]334 U.S. 558.   [46]336 U.S. 77.

affirmed a conviction under a statute prohibiting sound-trucks that emitted "raucous" noises, which the state court seemed to have construed to mean "all sound-trucks." In this case both the majority and the minority scattered in reasoning.

On the whole, the facts presented by the state cases—at least where something other and lesser than preventing the overthrow of the government is the asserted state interest—vary so widely that generalization is difficult. The differing philosophies and tendencies are not hard to identify. It is possible either to view in a friendly way any justification urged for suppression of speech, and (as in Beauharnais) any analogical line of reasoning that supports such suppression, or to come to such justificatory material with a strong set of mind against it. Both these attitudes are prior to the detailed analysis of each case, although they need not invariably determine the result of such analysis.

In New York Times Co. v. Sullivan (1964),[47] the Court for the first time considered the effect of the free-expression guarantees on private suits for libel. The Alabama courts had awarded damages to a city official in Montgomery who claimed his official conduct had been libelously criticized in an advertisement printed by the defendant newspaper. The Court held that the right of free expression prevails even against private libel actions, and protects the right to criticize officials in regard to their official conduct, unless "actual malice"—something like either actual knowledge of the falsity of the published statements, or reckless disregard of their accuracy—be shown.

Free Speech as a Relational Right. A prior question concerning all the stated cases is raised by the latent difficulty, already mentioned, of applying the First Amendment to the states.

"Liberty" can be taken away by a state, by "due process of law"; that phrase is commonly said to mean, as a substantive matter, that legislation must not be "arbitrary," that it must be possible for a rational man to believe it is instrumentally related to one of the permissible objects of government (see p. 78). The Gitlow opinion, wherein the Fourteenth Amendment "liberty" was first extended to free speech (see p. 77), proceeds on just this theory, and upholds the New York statute because such "reasonable relation" is found; it is ironic that the Gitlow decision should be relied on in Dennis, which, since it concerned a federal law, involved the First Amendment itself and had nothing to do with "due process." Later cases on state laws have imposed a stricter requirement. It has sometimes seemed that the Court has forgotten all about "due process," as though the states were subject to the First Amendment of its own force. But a difficulty is not overcome by being ignored.

As we saw above (p. 78), "due process" has for a long time called for a ranking of interests, and free speech has a very high claim. But it would be satisfying to be able to state a viable theory outside the "due process" clause for requiring, as a matter of federal constitutional law, that the states, within a wide range at least, respect freedom of utterance.

[47]376 U.S. 254.

Such a possibility may be latent in another line of reasoning altogether. The very existence of a national government—maintaining a judiciary, conducting elections, receiving petitions, resting on public opinion—may imply that the people who form its constituency possess rights that inhere in their relationship with it. One of these must be some measure of freedom of discussion. To start with the most obvious case, the Constitution provides for the popular election of congressmen. It is hard to think that, even if the subject of free speech were not mentioned in the Constitution, a state could validly forbid the public discussion of the merits of candidates for Congress.

But discussion of their merits, where it is most useful, involves discussion of all issues which may be involved (or which anyone may wish to see involved) in the contest. And in a continuing political society the confinement of discussion to election time, and to the positions of the candidates, is an untenable restriction; federal legislation, or problems which may lead to it, are among the matters people do discuss and are expected to discuss as members of a national polity like ours. It is maintainable, then, that state interference with the discussion of any topic which is or may be the subject of federal political action, including constitutional amendment, interferes with the most vital of all political relations between the government and the people of the Union.

The protection foreshadowed by this theory could be wide. Opinions on potentially federal subjects need not be held entitled to federal protection only when the speaker or writer is conscious of this federal orientation; the vague undirected complaint, the assailing of felt abuse without thought of remedy, is a valuable part of political life, the raw stuff on which the political process works. To protect speech and writing that contribute in any way to opinion-formation within the federal polity is no more a strain on doctrine than is the subjection to congressional regulation of activities substantially connected with interstate commerce, or the inference that excludes the states from burdening that commerce. Commerce among the states goes to the national economic life, but the traffic of ideas, beliefs, complaints, and hopes within the states goes to the political soul of the nation.[48]

The First Amendment, again, confirms this, without being crudely "incorporated" anywhere. It states the high national interest in free speech, assembly, and petition, as components in the nation's political process. Its function is, however, only corroborative. Our federal polity is a public-opinion polity; whatever kills the expression of opinion frustrates its assumed working. This would be true even if there were no First Amendment.

Although it has not been decisively rejected, this theory of national protection of free discussion as against the states has not been sanctioned by judicial decision. Generally, counsel and Court have been content to accept the Gitlow formula without worrying about the "due process" problem. As we saw above (p. 82), this may be partly because the Fourteenth Amendment "privileges and immunities" guarantee protects only "citizens of the United States," whereas the "due process" clause shields "persons," including aliens.

---

[48]See Brandeis' dissent in Gilbert v. Minnesota, 254 U.S. 325 (1920).

It has been thought that the connection of free speech to the implied relations between the federal government and its constituents would leave aliens unprotected.[49]

But the present line of thought is only suggested by the "privileges and immunities" clause, and does not rest on it. The relations of the federal government are with the *people*; there is no reason to limit that term to any less than all the people lawfully in the country. The decision by Congress that an alien may live here is an acceptance of a political relation with him. It is our traditional expectation that aliens may one day be voters. They are our eyes to the rest of the world. Their discontents have been a subject of active federal interest. They are counted in the enumeration for apportioning representatives in Congress. The state of opinion among them is a part of that political life with which the nation deals.

The reader may if he likes take the foregoing discussion as a sample of the speculation that makes or mars constitutional discourse when judicial settlement has not occurred. If we draw back to the preferred juristic style of our legal culture—that of founding constitutional protection on exegesis of text rather than on discernment of implication, on the written rather than on the unwritten Torah—the considerations just put forward support the two canons of interpretation needed to give wide protection to freedom of utterance. If this freedom goes to the national political life, then the First Amendment, limiting the national power, has a claim on the broadest construction—a claim to be interpreted as widely as the commerce clause. For the same reason, freedom of utterance has as high standing as any interest in that ranking of values which, as we have seen (pp. 79 ff.) is a part of the judicial work of interpreting the Fourteenth Amendment's "due process" guarantee running against the states.

The Weight of the Free-Speech Interest. Throughout this section the master problem has been seen to be the extent to which freedom of utterance must yield to competing values. Freedom of speech, say some, is an "absolute"; others seem to think that the judicial task in free speech cases is merely one of ascertaining whether arguably rational grounds exist for the suppressive measure. "Free speech" cannot be an "absolute" in the purest sense; no society could exist in which anyone could say whatever he chose— "Grimquack Cures Cancer"; "No, dear, I'm not married"; "Let's go down right now and assassinate Mayor Dinwiddie." But this easy demonstration quite fails to prove that free speech on matters of political opinion has no more than a "value" to be "balanced" against other "values" in an even-handed way. "Thou shalt not kill" is not an "absolute"—but it is possible to approach the question of killing in a far different frame of mind from that in which one approaches the question of severance of social relations.[50] Abstention from torture would be held by very few people to be a rule

---

[49]See Mr. Justice Stone, concurring in Hague v. C.I.O., 307 U.S. 496 (1939).

[50]I owe the analogy (with some difference, since he instances the First Commandment) to Pastor George Koski of Gloucester, Massachusetts (private correspondence). It shows that it is possible to approach alleged *ex necessitate* qualifications to a solemnly regarded command with an awed reluctance very far from what is usually meant by "balancing."

from which no variation could ever be proper—if, say, a man knew where a kidnapped child was hidden, and the child needed a tetanus shot right away, and the man would not tell. But to most people the justification of torture is outside systematic discourse. To some, the suppression of utterance—putting a man in prison for saying what he thinks—is so obscene a violation of human personality, so obstructive to political and social life, that the considerations requisite to justify it ought to be of about the same weight as those that would justify the administration of torture.[51]

IMMUNITY FROM RACIAL DISCRIMINATION

Before the Segregation Regime. Our most agonizing social and legal problem is racism. It goes back to the beginning. But relevant legal development covers just a hundred years; the Negro before the Civil War had few rights, and after it a new start was made. The pre-Civil War position is summed up in the Dred Scott[52] holding that even the free Negro was not a citizen.

Three new amendments followed the war. The Thirteenth abolished slavery. Abolition has stuck, in fact as well as in name; the peripheral problems merge into those of the working population in general.[53] Issues under the Fourteenth and the Fifteenth still burn.

The relevant parts of the Fourteenth are at page 75, *supra*; the Fifteenth reads:

> AMENDMENT XV. Section 1. The right of citizens of the United States to vote shall not be denied or abridged by the United States or by any State on account of race, color, or previous condition of servitude.
>
> Section 2. The Congress shall have power to enforce this article by appropriate legislation.

These amendments open two possibilities of legal action against racism. The first section of each pronounces a rule of constitutional law, against which state laws and other official actions must be judged by the courts. Secondly, each amendment authorizes Congress to pass implementing legislation. Congress has passed some such laws—following the Civil War, and again within the last few years (see p. 102, *infra*). The courts have had to judge the constitutionality of these congressional acts. The constitutional

---

[51]See C. L. Black, Jr., "Mr. Justice Black, the Supreme Court, and the Bill of Rights," *Harper's Magazine*, February, 1961.

[52]Scott v. Sanford, 19 How. (60 U.S.) 393 (1857).

[53]The recent decision in Jones v. Mayer, 392 U.S. 409 (1968), opens what may be a new head of federal legislative and judicial treatment of racial discrimination. Interpreting an 1866 law on prohibiting racial discrimination in housing, the Court held the law constitutional under the *Thirteenth* Amendment, on the ground that exclusion from housing was one of the "badges and incidents" of slavery. It is quite clear that such exclusion is not the *only* "badge or incident" of slavery, and the decision therefore suggests that Congress (and perhaps the Court too) has powers over racial discrimination under the Thirteenth Amendment as well as under the Fourteenth.

warrant of any such law lies in its claim to be "appropriate legislation" for "enforcing" the first section of one (or both) of the amendments. Thus, both judicial tasks—that of judging whether state laws transgress the first sections of the two amendments, and that of judging whether some act of Congress is warranted by the amendments—involve interpretation of the substantive first sections. The two types of cases are therefore interconnected by multiple ties of concept.

A clarifying division of the cases falls between those which do and those which do not involve voting. Roughly, this line runs between the two amendments, but the Fourteenth has had some impact on the voting problem.

The first section of the Fourteenth Amendment established Negro citizenship, putting Dred Scott to rest. The "privileges and immunities" clause has so far not meant much to the Negro. The "due process" clause has no specific racial application. The "equal protection" clause is the one most often applied to combat racism.

The Slaughterhouse Cases (1873),[54] the earliest Supreme Court decision construing the Fourteenth Amendment, held that a state could lawfully create a monopoly in slaughtering, a holding not important to us here. But the Court, in delivering its judgment, confirms an inference which the roughest knowledge of history would ground:

> We repeat, then, in the light of this recapitulation of events, almost too recent to be called history, but which are familiar to us all; and on the most casual examination of the language of these amendments, no one can fail to be impressed with the one pervading purpose found in them all . . . we mean the freedom of the slave race, the security and firm establishment of that freedom, and the protection of the newly-made freeman and citizen from the oppressions of those who had formerly exercized unlimited dominion over him. . . .
>
> . . . [I]t is necessary to look to the purpose which we have said was the pervading spirit of them all, the evil which they were designed to remedy, and the process of continued addition to the Constitution, until that purpose was supposed to be accomplished, as far as constitutional law can accomplish it.

In Strauder v. West Virginia (1880)[55] it was held that the amendment protected a Negro's right to trial by a jury selected without racial bias. The Court strongly restated the utterance of the Slaughterhouse opinion, saying of the Fourteenth Amendment:

> . . . What is this but declaring that the law in the States shall be the same for the black as for the white; that all persons, whether colored or white, shall stand equal before the laws of the States, and, in regard to the colored race, for whose protection the amendment was primarily designed, that no discrimination shall be made against them by law because of their color? The words of the amendment . . . contain a necessary implication of a positive immunity, or right, most valuable to the colored race,—the right to exemption from unfriendly legislation

---

[54]16 Wall. (83 U.S.) 36.   [55]100 U.S. 303.

against them distinctively as colored,—exemption from legal discriminations, implying inferiority in civil society, lessening the security of their
enjoyment of the rights which others enjoy, and discriminations which
are steps towards reducing them to the condition of a subject race.

. . . The very fact that colored people are singled out and expressly
denied by a statute all right to participate in the administration of the
law . . . is practically a brand upon them, affixed by the law, an assertion
of their inferiority, and a stimulant to that race prejudice which is an
impediment to securing to individuals of the race that equal justice
which the law aims to secure to all others. . . .

The Fourteenth Amendment makes no attempt to enumerate the
rights it is designed to protect. It speaks in general terms, and those are
as comprehensive as possible. . . .

This language (concurred in by 7 members of the Court, at a time
when the adoption of the amendment was a fresh memory) read the invoked
protections in the most general terms, and forcefully brought within the
amendment's ban even that discrimination which amounts to a "brand," or
an "assertion . . . of inferiority," as well as those which "lessen . . . security"
or are "steps towards" inferiority. If the Court had persisted in this early
reading, judicial protection against racism would have come earlier.

The Court later drew back, as we shall see. An intervening development, however, greatly disappointed those who trusted in the efficacy of
the Fourteenth Amendment—a development that had to do not with the
breadth of protection against discrimination by public authorities, but with
the problem whether such authorities were acting at all.

The Fourteenth Amendment prohibited action by the states: "No State
shall. . . ." In the Civil Rights Cases of 1883,[56] the Court held that an act
of Congress, prohibiting racial discrimination by innkeepers, common carriers,
and theaters, was not authorized by the Fourteenth Amendment, and hence
was unconstitutional. "State action," it was said, must be shown, before the
amendment may be invoked. The practical effect was denial of protection to
Negroes, where the infringement of their rights could be classified as technically "private," and where the state merely permitted such infringement.

The correctness of this holding was not as obvious as the majority
opinion makes it seem. Railroads and other common carriers had often been
referred to as instruments of the state, and enjoyed subsidies and "eminent
domain" rights which could be justified on no other view. Innkeepers were,
under the common law, required to serve all comers. More generally, the
states were forbidden, under the Fourteenth Amendment, to "deny equal
protection." The most obvious way to "deny protection" is to refrain from
acting; "state action" is an inapt phrase for this clause at least. The Civil
Rights Cases, like many decisions in which the reasoning is superficially
simple, plowed problems under. But it was a long time before the formally
"private" discrimination could be effectively questioned, however clear it was
that the whole moral (and even legal) authority of the state as polity and
community was behind it. The Civil Rights Cases principle, as it was com-

[56]109 U.S. 3.

monly received, protected from federal control even such practices as lynching and intimidation; the community could enforce a racist regime, so long as the state, in form, did no more than silently smile.

Segregation. Against this background, in 1896, came the landmark case of Plessy v. Ferguson.[57] Louisiana had passed a law (in the new pattern of racism) providing that white and colored were to travel on railroads in "equal but separate accommodations." ("State action" was no problem, for a state law was involved.) "Segregation" had entered the scene, and was to be the dominant issue for many years. The Court cited considerable state-court precedent for its decision upholding this law; none of this was binding, and some of it antedated the Fourteenth Amendment. The Court's efforts to find authority for what was in fact a new ruling led it into unusual dealings with its own past decisions. In Railroad Company v. Brown (1873),[58] it had held that segregation of passengers was "discrimination," and so infringed the congressional charter given to a railroad. To decide as it did in Plessy the Court had to find "equality" in the imposition of what it had squarely held to be "discrimination" in Brown. On the other hand, a case[59] in which the Plessy question had not been raised or decided—in which the Court had expressly said it was not deciding it—was described by the Plessy Court as, "indeed, almost directly in point."

But the most surprising passage, in all its bearings, is this:

> . . . The argument also assumes that social prejudices may be overcome by legislation, and that equal rights cannot be secured to the negro except by an enforced commingling of the two races. We cannot accept this proposition. If the two races are to meet upon terms of social equality, it must be the result of natural affinities, a mutual appreciation of each other's merits and a voluntary consent of individuals. . . .

This thought was more than problematical in application, since the law under consideration in Plessy was one which, within its range, *forbade* the two races to "meet upon terms of social equality," whatever their sentiments of "mutual appreciation," or however heartily two passengers of different races might give "voluntary consent" to sitting together. The question in Plessy was not whether "social prejudices may be overcome by legislation," but whether they may validly be fostered and reinforced by legislation.

The logical heart of the matter is found in the following language:

> We consider the underlying fallacy of the plaintiff's argument to consist in the assumption that the enforced separation of the two races stamps the colored race with a badge of inferiority. If this be so, it is not by reason of anything found in the act, but solely because the colored race chooses to put that construction upon it. . . .

---

[57]163 U.S. 537.   [58]17 Wall. (84 U.S.) 445.
[59]Louisville, etc. Ry. v. Miss., 133 U.S. 587 (1890).

This was the real issue in the Plessy case: Did segregation or did it not have the public meaning of an assertion of inferiority of the Negro race? If it did, then forcing Negroes to undergo a daily regime which constituted an "assertion of [their] inferiority" could not (as a matter of common sense as well as under the language quoted above from the Strauder[60] case) be consonant with a thoroughgoing "equal protection of the laws." To be insulted is a hurt, recognized as such in law long before the Fourteenth Amendment; to be denominated inferior by the state, whether in words or by enforced gesture, is to be treated unequally by the state.

The Court's assertion, in the language just quoted, is that no such public meaning attached to segregation—that it was rather the oversensitivity of the Negroes that read such a meaning into it. There is no suggestion of the basis for this conclusion in social psychology. Justice Harlan, in dissent, insisted that it was wrong; a Kentucky man's difficulties with it are comprehensible.

The assault on the "separate but equal" formula was slow in coming along. The first breach was opened in Buchanan v. Warley (1917).[61] A Louisville ordinance made it a crime for anyone, white or Negro, to move into a residential block occupied by a majority of the other race; the eventual result would be the creation of permanently "Negro" and "white" parts of town, maintained by law. The scheme was formally "equal" in its incidence on both racial groups. But it was too much for the Court; the ordinance was invalidated. The presence of a "property" right was emphasized. But there was really no sound ground of distinction from Plessy v. Ferguson; "commingling" was the evil aimed at in both cases, and there was no good reason why the state that might prohibit Negroes and whites from sitting next to one another on trains might not prohibit their living next to one another, or take lesser steps in the same direction. Buchanan v. Warley lay in radical disconformity on the Plessy doctrine.

But Plessy was far from overruled. Although the Supreme Court did not specifically reaffirm its doctrine, as a matter of square holding, in the years after Buchanan v. Warley, it was generally assumed to be correct, and segregation by law became the dominant expression of racism.

The slow general attack was by way of the "equal" part of the "separate but equal" formula. The "equality," more often than not, was equality by postulation only. In schools, for example, segregating states generally spent on Negro education a minor fraction of the amount *per capita* spent on white education. Some facilities, moreover, could not practicably be duplicated; Missouri v. Canada (1938)[62] is an example. Missouri had only one state law school. The Supreme Court held that the state's giving a Negro funds to study law in a non-segregating neighbor state did not relieve it of the duty to admit him to the law school of his own state. The fact that Negroes rarely used sleeping cars was not accepted as a sufficient excuse for failing to provide for the furnishing of such accommodations to Negroes desiring them;[63] "from him that hath not it shall be taken away" was not accepted as a sufficient reason for discrimination.

In the education cases the question slowly began to form itself: Can

---

[60]*Supra*, pp. 94–95.   [61]245 U.S. 60.   [62]305 U.S. 337.
[63]McCabe v. A.T. & S.F. R.R., 235 U.S. 151 (1914).

"separate" education really be "equal"? A milestone was Sweatt v. Painter (1950).[64] The Negro petitioner, excluded from the University of Texas Law School, was offered legal education at a "school," established for the purpose, with no faculty or library of its own and no accreditation. While the case was wending its way up, a somewhat better Negro law school was established, but one still greatly inferior to the University of Texas Law School. This inferiority might have sufficed for decision. But the Court added some highly significant language:

> . . . The law school, the proving ground for legal learning and practice, cannot be effective in isolation from the individuals and institutions with which the law interacts. Few students and no one who has practiced law would choose to study in an academic vacuum, removed from the interplay of ideas and the exchange of views with which the law is concerned. . . .

This line of thought struck between the ribs of segregation, for it recognized that exclusion from the mainstream of community life was itself incompatible with equality, at least in respect of many activities and callings.

In the companion McLaurin[65] case (1950), the Court went even further. McLaurin was admitted as a Negro graduate student at the University of Oklahoma, but was required to sit apart from his white fellows. Of these restrictions, the Court said:

> . . . But they signify that the State, in administering the facilities it affords for professional and graduate study, sets McLaurin apart from the other students. The result is that appellant is handicapped in his pursuit of effective graduate instruction. Such restrictions impair and inhibit his ability to study, to engage in discussions and exchange views with other students, and, in general, to learn his profession. . . .

This is 170 degrees from Plessy v. Ferguson. After the Sweatt and McLaurin decisions, the clock began to tick on segregation.

It struck in the School Segregation Cases[66] of 1954, which outlawed the practice altogether in state-supported schools. In decisions soon after, other forms of segregation were outlawed.[67] There can be reasonable differences of view on the quality of the School Segregation opinion as written. It is not explicit or full on the reasons for regarding segregation as a harm. The cause is not far to seek. The question whether segregation of the Negro, as practiced in the United States, implies an "assertion of inferiority" (and so infringes the venerable and evidently sensible standard of Strauder v. West Virginia) is a question that can be answered only by reference to some pretty well-known facts about the history, society, and politics of the United States, and especially of one section. Those facts are not hidden; they

---

[64]339 U.S. 629.
[65]339 U.S. 637.
[66]Brown v. Bd. of Education of Topeka, 347 U.S. 483 (1954).
[67]E.g., New Orleans City Park Improvement Ass'n v. Detiege, 358 U.S. 54 (1958); Crayle v. Browder, 352 U.S. 903 (1956); Holmes v. Atlanta, 350 U.S. 879 (1955).

are known to all educated people.[68] Yet their recital is an unpleasant task, from which the Court might understandably (if not pardonably) shrink. Such reticence, if it existed, has no tendency to impeach the correctness of the decisions.

In a hundred years, then, our law has been through an impressive development; as a matter of law now, racial distinctions (including segregation) cannot exist in the United States. The remaining heavy problem is that of enforcement against resistance and evasion.

The Modern "State Action" Problem. Meanwhile, the "state action" problem, discussed above in connection with the Civil Rights Cases, has undergone significant exploration. The question whether, in any situation, governmental power has been so exerted as to bring constitutional guarantees into play is now seen to be one of great difficulty. The involvements of state power with nominally "private" patterns of activity are complex and various.

The breakthrough modern case is Shelley v. Kraemer (1948).[69] As we saw above, Buchanan v. Warley (1917) held that residential segregation by law was unconstitutional. To avoid the effect of this decision, "racial restrictive covenants" were widely entered into; property-owners in a neighborhood "covenanted" that they would not sell to Negroes, and that Negroes would never occupy the property. In many states these covenants, if properly recorded in a public office, were binding not only on the original covenantors but also on those who later took title to the property. The state courts would then enforce them by judicial orders forbidding (under penalty) sale to or occupancy by Negroes. In the Shelley case, a state court had issued such an injunction, ordering a Negro purchaser not to live in the house he had bought. If the state had by law forbidden his living there, "state action" would clearly have been involved and Buchanan v. Warley would have applied. Was there sufficient "state action" in the covenant pattern to make the Fourteenth Amendment applicable?

The Court held there was, in an opinion which did not satisfactorily explore the issues. It was stressed that judicial action—which of course is state action—was involved; but that would have been true if an injunction had been issued to halt a trespass on private residential property owned and occupied by the plaintiff, and it cannot be thought that the Fourteenth Amendment makes it unlawful for the resident owner of a house to choose the people who will enter.

On its facts, however, Shelley v. Kraemer differs widely from such a case. The Shelley injunction aided no one in excluding persons from his own land, but aimed at impressing a character on a neighborhood. In order to issue it, the state court had to find as a fact that the defendant was a Negro. A state-controlled machinery of recordation, in addition to the state judicial machinery, was involved. The "covenant" scheme was functionally equivalent to a racial zoning ordinance. It differed only formally from a statute making it illegal for a Negro to live in any neighborhood, if at some

---

[68]For a canvass of these, see C. L. Black, Jr., "The Lawfulness of the Segregation Decisions," 69 *Yale Law Journal* 421 (1960).
[69]334 U.S. 1.

time in the past the property-owners therein had unanimously voted that such residency was thenceforward to be unlawful. These facts and others have suggested to subsequent commentators more satisfactory explanations of the Shelley holding than the one the Court tendered.

The case only illustrated the modern "state action" problem. Where a union has governmental support as certified bargaining agent, it has been strongly hinted that constitutional guarantees apply.[70] Where a library, nominally "private," enjoys public support, "state action" in sufficient quantity has been found.[71] And of course, where the formally "private" arrangement is fraudulent, set up for the purpose of evading the Constitution, the same result is indicated.[72] (See the primary cases, discussed below.)

The "state action" doctrine, in racial discrimination cases, is now in a most fluid state. Strikingly, no recent Supreme Court case has squarely held that "state action" is *not* present, in a racial case, though sometimes decision on the issue has been avoided by recourse to alternative grounds,[73] or by denial of certiorari. "State action" has been found to exist: (1) where government property is leased to a restauranteur, who then excludes Negroes from his "private" restaurant;[74] (2) where a city ordinance commands restaurant segregation, even though the ordinance is clearly invalid, and even though it is not certain whether the store manager "would have acted as he did independent of the ordinance";[75] (3) where, after a city has long held and operated a park as trustee under a will requiring exclusion of Negroes, it is then sought, by the city's resignation and the substitution of "private" trustees, to maintain the all-white character of the park;[76] (4) where a state, having previously had in force a law prohibiting racial discrimination in the renting and sale of residential property, puts into force a constitutional amendment forbidding the future passage or enforcement of any such fair-housing law by the legislature or by any other statewide or local organ of government.[77] These cases all too meagerly sample the broad field of "state action."

Subjacent to all problems in this field is the master-question: "When can it be said that the power of government is significantly engaged in the act of racial discrimination which presents itself as formally private?" It is now abundantly clear that the formal privacy is not in itself enough to rebut the inference of "state action." Many are beginning to feel that "state action" always supports nominally "private" discrimination in some way, and that no warranted line can be drawn to immunize "private" racial discrimination on the ground that "no state action" is present. Most writers who take this position also maintain that other criteria, applied to interpreting the Fourteenth Amendment, may warrantably prevent any holding that private persons may not discriminate, even racially, in those spheres of life which are authenti-

[70]Steele v. Louisville & Nashville RR., 323 U.S. 192 (1944).
[71]Kerr v. Enoch Pratt Free Library, 149 Federal Reporter, 2d Series 212 (Fourth Circuit Court of Appeals, 1945), *certiorari denied*, 326 U.S. 721.
[72]Cooper v. Aaron, 358 U.S. 1 (1958).
[73]E.g., Bell v. Md., 378 U.S. 226 (1964).
[74]Burton v. Wilmington Parking Authority, 365 U.S. 715 (1961).
[75]Peterson v. Greenville, 373 U.S. 244 (1963).
[76]Evans v. Newton, 382 U.S. 296 (1966).
[77]Reitman v. Mulkey, 387 U.S. 369 (1967).

cally "private"—the personal social life, for example, as opposed to the generally public restaurant. On any view, close questions will arise; the current state of the subject is such that we can only await further clarification by the Supreme Court.

Racial Discrimination in Voting. The Fifteenth Amendment, up to a point, speaks with clarity. Racial discrimination by law, in regard to voting in regular elections, is outlawed. But a number of important questions remain: What can be done about private interference with voting? What is the position on "primaries"? How deeply will the Court go (or permit Congress to go) into hidden patterns of discrimination?

In *ex parte Yarbrough* (1884)[78] conviction was obtained under a statute making it a crime to "prevent by force, intimidation, or threat, any citizen who is lawfully entitled to vote" from supporting whom he chooses for President or Congress. The indictment had charged that the defendants conspired to intimidate a Negro in the exercise of his right to vote for a member of Congress. The question was whether the statute was constitutional, no "state action" being present. The Court held that Congress, under its power to regulate "Times, Places, and Manners" of congressional election, could make criminal such conduct as this, even on the part of private individuals. The right to vote in such elections was held to be derived from Article I of the Constitution, and so to be a proper subject of federal protection, against "private" as well as against "state" action. On the other hand, the Court gave a grudgingly narrow construction to some of the federal voting statutes, and invalidated others. For example, in U.S. v. Reese (1876),[79] federal penalization of interference with the right to vote was held too broad, since it was not expressly limited to interference on racial grounds. The Negro had the right to vote in the abstract, but his remedies were sparse and unreliable.

Even in principle, federal power to reach discrimination in primaries was long developing. These were (and to a diminished extent still are) the only meaningful elections in some states. In Nixon v. Herndon (1924),[80] it was held that racial exclusion by law from a state-conducted Democratic primary in Texas was obnoxious to the equal protection clause. The state response was to make the primaries nominally "private," leaving it to the good sense of Democratic party conventions and committees to exclude Negroes. The Court finally held that this would not serve.[81] In Terry v. Adams (1953),[82] a "once-removed" primary came to the Court; the "Jaybirds" (all the white Democrats in a Texas county) had their own pre-primary, the winners of which almost always won the regular Democratic primary and the general election. The Court, holding even this arrangement subject to the Constitution, decided that the Jaybird officials must let Negroes vote.

Much discourse was spent on these obvious frauds on the Constitution. Of the several doctrinal routes for getting at the Jaybirds (and other fraudulent primaries) perhaps the most satisfying (because it is the one that goes to the heart of the matter) is found in the last work of Judge Learned Hand, though he invoked the principle in another connection:

[78]110 U.S. 651.   [79]92 U.S. 214.   [80]273 U.S. 536.
[81]Smith v. Allwright, 321 U.S. 649 (1944).   [82]345 U.S. 461.

> For centuries it has been an accepted canon in interpretation of documents to interpolate into the text such provisions, although not expressed, as are essential to prevent the defeat of the venture at hand, . . .[83]

The technique suggested here must be reserved for great matters and clear need. Greater matter and clearer need never was than the problem of effective voting by millions of people. It is thoroughly reasonable to read into the Fifteenth Amendment the means of its own preservation from being brought to nothing by trickery.

Another means of depriving the Negro of the vote is that of imposing "qualifications" that bear only or chiefly on him, without mentioning skin color. The "grandfather clause" is typical. Oklahoma put in force a statute that (in part) limited voting to those whose ancestors could vote in 1866. Since Negroes could not vote in 1866, the "grandfather clause" was really a "No-Negro clause." The Court saw this, and struck it down.[84] The state acceded nominally, then set a two-week period for registration of all who could not meet the "grandfather" requirement, barring them forever after. This too the Court struck down,[85] as transparent subterfuge.

Much harder to deal with is the discriminatory administration of tests valid on their face. "Literacy" tests, or tests on "understanding the Constitution," are sometimes used to refuse registration to Negroes, while whites pass easily. Where the discrimination can be proved in court, it can be enjoined. But proof is not always easy; congressional remedies, as we shall see, have been found to be needed.

Congress Comes to the Court's Aid. The field of racial discrimination is one in which judicial review has worked well. One of the standard objections to vigorous use of the judicial power to protect constitutional rights has always been that the judiciary has little power to accomplish anything—that only the slow movement of social change, and the political acceptance of legislation, can have much effect on basic human rights. The progress of racial emancipation, slow as it is, is a mortal threat to this counsel of impotence. Almost solely because of judicial activism, up to quite recent times, segregation has been weakened in many states. Negroes are voting in greater numbers than ever. A great change has begun and progressed. And the Court's work has, so far as one can discern, been absolutely indispensable. The judicial power has done much, during years when Congress and the Presidents were doing as little as they could. Saddening as it is that legislative and executive action in this field has so often in the past turned out to be a blow swung through water, there was some fitness in the use of the judicial power, which speaks in the name of law, to deal with these matters.

Nevertheless, vigorous congressional action was needed, and Congress has begun assuming its responsibilities. The Civil Rights Act of 1964[86] and

---

[83]Learned Hand, *The Bill of Rights* (Cambridge, Mass.: Harvard University Press, 1958), p. 14.

[84]Guinn v. U.S., 238 U.S. 347 (1915).   [85]Lane v. Wilson, 307 U.S. 268 (1939).

[86]78 U.S. *Statutes at Large* 241.

the Voting Rights Act of 1965[87] are the two most important pieces of modern legislation.

The 1964 Act covered a wide range of topics—voting, discrimination in places of public accommodation, segregation in public facilities, schools, and federally assisted programs, and equality in employment opportunity. One of its most important effects was its giving express congressional approval and support to the epoch-making segregation decisions; these now rest not only on the Court's authority, but on the authority of every branch of the national government.

Title II of the Act very significantly affects the practice of racial discrimination in public establishments. It is provided, for example, that no restaurant that "serves or offers to serve" interstate travelers, or derives a substantial proportion of its food from interstate commerce, may discriminate on racial grounds. It is to be observed, first, that Congress is here relying on its commerce power, and, secondly, that the criteria stated, though drawn on a commerce-power theory, will cover the great majority of all public restaurants. In consequence, the "state action" question, discussed above, will probably no longer arise as to discrimination by such establishments; such discrimination is now forbidden whether supported by "state action" or not. The constitutionality of this Title was upheld by the Court, in two cases already mentioned in their commerce-clause context. (See *supra*, p. 31.)

The Voting Rights Act of 1965 drastically attacks the problem of racial discrimination in voting. Its coverage formula, and the "triggering" devices that bring it into operation, virtually assure that it will operate almost entirely in states and parts of states where racial exclusion from voting is a serious problem. It provides for the suspension of various "tests or devices" which Congress found to have been used to effect discrimination. It provides for the use of federal officials to register voters, where the Attorney General finds that good faith on the part of state registrars cannot be relied on. The Act was upheld by the Court, as a valid exercise of Congress' power under §2 of the Fifteenth Amendment, in South Carolina v. Katzenbach.[88]

PROCEDURAL REGULARITY AND FAIRNESS

The Field of Problems. The criminal law is the ultimate weapon of society; its proper use is the most imperative of society's duties. Fairness in procedure has enjoyed constitutional status with us since the beginning, even though its political bearing is not as evident as those of intellectual freedom and immunity from irrational discrimination.

Before a law is broken, there must be a law. How clearly must it describe the forbidden conduct? If conduct designated in a statute solely as "anti-social" may be punished, how will the citizen know whether some act he considers performing will make him eligible for the penitentiary? How can the judge before whom the charge is brought make a rational decision whether the law has been broken?[89]

---

[87]79 *id.* at 437.   [88]383 U.S. 301 (1966).   [89]See Lanzetta v. N.J., 306 U.S. 451 (1939).

Before a man can be punished he must be arrested and held. At this time (or later) he may make damaging admissions or a full confession; it is a chief aim of police procedure to bring this about. Are there any limits on the later use of these statements to support a conviction? Are they to be admissible in evidence in every case? In every case except where physical torture has been employed? Only when there has been a prompt arraignment before a magistrate?[90]

Houses, cars, persons, may be searched. When may the evidence so procured be admitted? Always? Only when a warrant was first obtained?[91]

Some formal accusation must be made, or there is no charge to try. By whom? By a grand jury? By any policeman? (Even to be charged and put to trial, aside from intangible detriments, can ruin most people financially.)[92]

Can the accused call witnesses?[93] Will the state pay their travel fees? Must the trial be public?[94] Must the prosecuting attorney be "fair," in some special sense, or is he just another lawyer out to win his case?[95]

Has the accused a right to a lawyer? From the time of the arrest? At the trial only? Only if he can pay him?[96]

Is there a right to appeal? For those who can pay for it, or for anybody?[97]

Has publicity before the trial made fairness impossible?[98] Has publicity during the trial had the same effect?[99]

These questions only sample the field. To focus on any one of them is to perceive a crucial issue of fairness. Behind each is a body of practice and decisions. We can discuss here only some general issues, with a few examples.

The Functions of the Supreme Court. Constitutional law, enunciated by the Court, cannot produce thorough-going procedural regularity and fairness. Most unlawful police procedures are lost in the poverty of the victims; most irregularity and bias is probably masked behind the plea of "guilty" and the silent departure for prison. A practice may be judicially condemned in a dramatic, hard-fought case; this does not mean that it is generally abandoned.

Still, the enforcement of standards in cases where they can be invoked probably has some good effect. Guidance is given to those law-enforcement officers (hopefully the majority) who want to work within the law. Those otherwise minded—and they are certainly numerous—are put on notice that conviction may be imperiled if minimum standards are disregarded. And the educational effect on the community as a whole may be salutary. In this work the Supreme Court serves three important functions. Two concern the operations of the federal government only; one concerns the states.

[90]See Fikes v. Alabama, 352 U.S. 191 (1957); Miranda v. Arizona, 384 U.S. 436 (1966).
[91]See infra, pp. 107–109.
[92]See U.S. v. Moreland, 258 U.S. 433 (1922); Hurtado v. Calif., 110 U.S. 516 (1884).
[93]Amendment VI.
[94]See Re Oliver, 333 U.S. 257 (1948).
[95]Alcorta v. Texas, 355 U.S. 28 (1957).
[96]Cases infra, pp. 106–107.
[97]Griffin v. Illinois, 351 U.S. 12 (1956).
[98]Rideau v. La., 373 U.S. 723 (1963).
[99]Sheppard v. Maxwell, 384 U.S. 333 (1966).

The first, although not strictly dealing with constitutional guarantees, is so interwoven in practice with the Court's constitutional function that it must be considered here. The Supreme Court heads the federal judiciary; it may ultimately review every conviction in any federal court (see p. 11, *supra*). The Court therefore finally interprets all federal laws concerning procedure, and—where no congressional enactments govern—must pronounce ultimately on the rightness of procedures followed in the lower federal courts. In this capacity the Court has been said to possess a general "power of supervision over the administration of justice in the Federal courts. . . ."[100] Congress has recognized and regularized this position by conferring on the Court power to make procedural rules for the lower federal courts; the current Federal Rules of Criminal Procedure are of this origin.

In performing this first function, the Court need make no constitutional decisions. It must only decide—as any court of last resort must—on the propriety of challenged practices, using the whole set of legal materials—acts of Congress, applicable rules promulgated by itself, and such traditional or "common-law" matter as may be available.

The second function is sharply differentiated in theory. The Court must enforce, even against acts of Congress, the commands of the Constitution respecting federal criminal procedure. These are collected, chiefly, in the Bill of Rights (see p. 75). "Unreasonable searches and seizures" are prohibited. Grand jury indictment is required for "infamous crimes." Double jeopardy, compulsory self-incrimination, and deprivation of life, liberty, or property "without due process of law" are forbidden. Jury trial, clarity of accusation, confrontation of witnesses, and other rights, are guaranteed.

In practice, the above two functions tend to merge. When a particular procedural step in a federal court is condemned, the Court does not always have to decide whether it acts because the Constitution has been violated, or because applicable law and rules have not been followed. This issue must be faced only when Congress has clearly set up the questioned procedure. Generally, Congress has been content to leave the administration of justice to the courts.

In some cases, however, the problem occurs. In Boyd v. U.S. (1886),[101] for example, Congress had clearly provided that the defendant in a revenue forfeiture proceeding must either produce such books and records of his own as the prosecuting attorney required or suffer an adverse finding on the allegation which the government proposed to prove by the requested records. The Court held this unconstitutional, as an unreasonable search and seizure and as a requirement of self-incrimination.

A third function of the Court has quite a different bearing. The "due process" and "equal protection" clauses of the Fourteenth Amendment govern *state* criminal proceedings; a claimed transgression of these by a state is ground for appellate jurisdiction in the Supreme Court (*supra*, p. 11) as well as for *habeas corpus* proceedings in the lower federal courts (p. 47), reviewable by the Supreme Court.

We have seen (p. 76) that the Fourteenth Amendment has been held not formally to "incorporate" the federal Bill of Rights; the specific provisions

[100]Thiel v. So. Pac. Co., 328 U.S. 217 (1946).   [101]116 U.S. 616.

of the latter do not run against the states. The Fourteenth Amendment question, the Court once said, is whether the particular Bill of Rights provision is ". . . of the very essence of a scheme of ordered liberty."[102] But, as we have seen (supra, p. 76), this formulation no longer realistically describes the Court's perception of the relation between the Bill of Rights and the Fourteenth Amendment—unless it be on the theory that whatever is bad enough to have been picked out for condemnation in the Bill of Rights is by the same token bad enough to fall outside the "scheme of ordered liberty." "Incorporation," rejected in theory, is followed in practice as to most of the Bill of Rights guarantees against oppressive governmental practices in administration of the criminal law. The result is that, for the most part, constitutional decisions with regard to fairness in criminal procedure are interchangeably applicable to federal and state criminal proceedings.

A Few Problem Areas. We can take up only a few cases which exhibit the Court's performance in its triple role. We may start with the problem of "right to counsel"—in some sense the right that is basic to all others, since it insures (ideally) that other rights will be claimed.

The path-breaking modern case is Johnson v. Zerbst (1938).[103] The trial was in a federal court, and was therefore subject to the Bill of Rights, and specifically to the Sixth Amendment right "to have the Assistance of Counsel." The accused had been unable to employ counsel, and the question was whether the district court should have appointed a lawyer for him. The Supreme Court gave the Sixth Amendment its literal interpretation, holding that even those who cannot pay must be furnished counsel in federal criminal cases.

The question that had to arise next was the extent to which this right to counsel was, as a matter of *federal* right, available in *state* trials, as a part of Fourteenth Amendment "due process." The Court's interim answer was for a while a compromise. At least in non-capital cases, the more individuated rule stemming from Betts v. Brady (1942)[104] prevailed; counsel in state criminal cases must be furnished only where special circumstances make procedure without counsel unfair.

The trouble with this rule was that it stated a distinction on only one side of which real cases fall. The facts of being poor and charged with crime are themselves special circumstances which make any man need a lawyer badly. The Court did at last take note of the fact that the Betts v. Brady rule cannot be made to work fairly, and that, at a minimum, fairness in procedure requires the assistance of counsel.[105]

Right to counsel, once recognized, could not be confined to the time of trial. In the highly controversial case of Miranda v. Arizona (1966),[106] the question was the extent to which a suspect was to be entitled to have the advice and assistance of counsel during that police questioning which is typically the first stage in the process by which criminal liability is imposed. At this stage, of course, the right-to-counsel problem is inextricably tied up

[102]Palko v. Conn., 302 U.S. 319 (1937).   [103]304 U.S. 458.   [104]316 U.S. 455.
[105]Gideon v. Wainwright, 372 U.S. 335 (1963).   [106]384 U.S. 436.

with the problem of self-incrimination, because the presence of a lawyer is the most efficacious guard against self-incrimination. The Court held that "the need for counsel to protect the Fifth Amendment privilege comprehends not merely a right to consult with counsel prior to questioning, but also to have counsel present during any questioning, if the defendant so desires." The Court said that the accused must be fully and effectively notified of this right, and that, if he cannot afford a lawyer, the state must furnish him one.

It has been said that this decision will seriously hamper law-enforcement; police depend, it is claimed, on admissions and confessions procured by the method of in-custody interrogation, and any lawyer worth his salt will necessarily advise his client to be silent. Empirical studies of police practices, since Miranda, cast doubt on the catastrophic nature of the consequences of the case.[107] Only time will finally tell how serious these are.

Underlying Miranda, though not expressed in the opinion, is something which marks the great majority of cases dealing with police methods. The legislatures and Congress, by and large, have not been willing to face and solve the problems, in general laws defining what the police may do, and what rights suspects may claim. The consequence is that, in deciding cases of the Miranda type, the Court is not overturning a prior legislative judgment of social necessity and wisdom, but is overturning only the judgment of the police. The Court's activity in this field might have been very different if, for example, Congress had enacted (under its power to enforce the Fourteenth Amendment) a code governing in-custody interrogation, imposing limits on police practice and by implication stating a national understanding that police action within those limits was permissible. The absence of any such balancing of the respective claims of order and freedom, by some organ of government competent (as the police chief surely is not) to balance them, would seem to constitute a radical want of "due process of law"—because there is commonly no "law" at all dealing with the matter. It might be that explicit legislative attention to these problems, and search for their workable solution, would gradually change the present unfortunate situation, in which the Court is often the only authority available for dealing with these matters, unless they are to be left wholly to police discretion—a solution few would favor upon seeing it explicitly formulated.

The "search and seizure" cases present another interesting pattern. The Bill of Rights ban (Amendment IV) is against "unreasonable searches and seizures." Generally, a search without a warrant is "unreasonable" unless very strong grounds justify it.[108] Many police searches make no pretense of being "reasonable" in this sense. What are the consequences of the "unreasonable" search?

It has always been clear that the only way to discourage unlawful searches by police is to exclude the evidence so procured from the trial, and to reverse convictions where it has been admitted. The police will not enforce the rules of lawful search against themselves; the problem arises

[107]"Interrogations in New Haven: The Impact of Miranda," 76 *Yale Law Journal* 1519 (1967).
[108]McDonald v. U.S., 335 U.S. 451 (1948).

only when they have already broken those rules. It has also seemed to many that proceeding to conviction on the basis of evidence unconstitutionally procured made the courts parties to wrong, putting the judiciary in an untenable moral position. The crucial question has then been whether this effect—exclusion—was to follow on a judicial finding of illegality in procuring evidence.

In Weeks v. U.S. (1914)[109] the Court held that, in a *federal* prosecution, evidence procured in violation of the Fourth Amendment was to be excluded.

Did the Fourteenth Amendment command the same result in *state* trials? In Wolf v. Colorado (1949)[110] the defendant was arrested by state police and his office searched without a warrant; he was later convicted, in state court, on the evidence so procured. The Supreme Court held that this search (which it found not justified by the circumstances) violated the Fourteenth Amendment, since ". . . security of one's privacy against arbitrary intrusion by the police is basic to a free society." Must the conviction based on evidence so procured be reversed? No (said the Court), although "due process" was offended by the search, the evidence need not be excluded. The "right" and its mode of enforcement were two different things. A dissent went to the practical point: "There is but one alternative to the rule of exclusion. That is no sanction at all. . . ."

Meanwhile another problem arose. In the Weeks case the Court, while insisting that evidence unlawfully seized by *federal* officers could not be admitted in a *federal* criminal trial, had said that evidence seized by *state* officers could be admitted in federal court; the Weeks Court noted that the Fourth Amendment made unlawful only searches and seizures by federal officials, and did not consider whether the Fourteenth Amendment condemned the actions of the state officers.

Difficulties early arose; where federal officers "cooperated," the Fourth Amendment taint was present, and the evidence was inadmissible.[111] And at last, with the decision in Wolf, the underpinnings of the rule were removed, for Wolf held (without practical effect, in the case itself) that Fourteenth Amendment "due process" *did* forbid wrongful searches on the part of state officials; if so, then a federal court could no more admit the illegally procured evidence than if it were turned up by the F.B.I. This was recognized by the whole Court in Elkins v. U.S. (1960).[112]

Finally, in Mapp v. Ohio (1961),[113] the circle of protection was completed. Wolf was overruled, and it was held that evidence procured by wrongful search and seizure was inadmissible in criminal proceedings in either state or federal courts:

> The ignoble shortcut to conviction left open to the State tends to destroy the entire system of constitutional restraints on which the liberties of the people rest. Having once recognized that the right to privacy embodied in the Fourth Amendment is enforceable against the States, and that the right to be secure against rude invasions of privacy

[109]232 U.S. 383.   [110]338 U.S. 25.   [111]See Lustig v. U.S., 338 U.S. 74 (1949).
[112]364 U.S. 206.   [113]367 U.S. 643.

by state officers is, therefore, constitutional in origin, we can no longer permit that right to remain an empty promise.

The Courts and Procedural Fairness. If all men were either criminals or angels, and if only angels were concerned in the administration of law, we would need no constitutional canons of fair procedure; these exist to neutralize, as far as may be, three factors, often working together: (1) the over-zeal of police and prosecutors; (2) the prejudices of the community; (3) the poverty and helplessness of nearly all defendants, relative to the vast resources of the state. It may be, as some say and many think, that almost all who are charged with crime are "guilty." It does not follow that this would be true if we relaxed our procedural safeguards, for it might then become easy and rewarding to charge with crime those who were not guilty. If all the water is on the right side of the dike, that is because the dike is there. And of course it is only an assumption that the innocent are rarely charged; to make it is to impute infallibility to a process all too human.

But what is it about these matters that raises them to the high political sphere of the Constitution? Most obviously, just as courage is the condition of every other virtue, fair procedure is a condition to every freedom. If men could be convicted of burglary without pretense of fairness, it would be simple to deal with people who uttered unpopular opinions as though they were burglars. Too, a widely diffused feeling that the lives and liberties of the people do not lie at the mercy of officialdom is a component of general satisfaction and security—among the highest political goods. In practice, the guarantee of fair procedure is an adjunct to the guarantee against discrimination on racial and other irrational grounds; harsh and arbitrary procedures have their maximum impact on minority groups, and the setting of minimum standards for all gives most help to those most disadvantaged.

But underneath all this, transcendent in importance, is the sheer national interest in justice, not as a means only, but as a good in itself. A conviction before a biased jury may be a threat to freedom of speech, to equality of citizens, or to some other evidently political interest. But, more than that, it always and intrinsically is an abomination. It is disgusting in itself, as well as productive of untoward consequences, that police should freely enter and search the house of any man they choose.

Our constitutional protections of procedural fairness and regularity are minimal; they fight uphill, and they do little if any more than hold their ground. As evidence procured by officers unlawfully breaking down a door is at last excluded from court, some new variation on the "dirty business"[114] of wiretapping is put to work. But the fact that the fight is waged, and that the Constitution provides weapons for this as for more evidently "political" ends, is one of the most striking signs of the commitment of our nation.

114Holmes, dissenting in Olmstead v. U.S., 277 U.S. 438 (1928).

To explore further

A good casebook is the most useful companion to the present work. The books that follow fully illustrate all matters here broached and contain abundant listings of further readings:

Paul A. Freund et al., *Constitutional Law: Cases and Other Problems*, 3rd ed. (Boston: Little, Brown, 1967). 2 vols.
Paul G. Kauper, *Constitutional Law: Cases and Materials*, 3rd ed. (Boston: Little, Brown, 1966).
Wm. B. Lockhart et al., *Constitutional Law: Cases, Comments, Questions*, 2nd ed. (St. Paul: West Publishing Co., 1967).

The standard history of the Court is Charles Warren, *The Supreme Court in United States History*, rev. ed. (Boston: Little, Brown, 1926). An acknowledged and influential classic is Paul A. Freund, *On Understanding the Supreme Court* (Boston: Little, Brown, 1949). Charles P. Curtis, *Lions under the Throne* (Boston: Houghton Mifflin, 1947), stresses the institutional place of the court; while Edmond A. Cahn (ed.), *Supreme Court and Supreme Law* (Bloomington, Ind.: Indiana University Press, 1954), is a symposium on vital issues. Charles L. Black, Jr., *The People and the Court* (New York: Macmillan, 1960; paperback ed., Prentice-Hall, 1967), will appeal particularly to those who are interested in a fuller development of the "activist" ideas in this book. Very much on the other side is Alexander M. Bickel, *The Least Dangerous Branch* (Indianapolis: Bobbs-Merrill, 1962). Some of the other ideas in this present book are expanded in Black, *Structure and Relationship in Constitutional Law* (Baton Rouge: Louisiana State University Press, 1969).

To cite all the articles pertinent to a book of this sort would consume far more space than we have available here. I shall mention three sources that are particularly valuable: *Index to Legal Periodicals*, issued serially in three-year cumulations, with frequent interim supplements, is the key to periodical literature. A wealth of material on all topics is in *Select Essays on Constitutional Law*, (Chicago: Foundation Press, 1938), 4 vols., and *Selected Essays on Constitutional Law, 1938–1962* (St. Paul: West Publishing Co., 1963).

INDEX

Freedom of the press (*see* Freedom of
expression)
Full faith and credit, obligations between
states, 50–51

"Grandfather" clause, 102

H*abeas corpus*, 47
Hand, Learned, *Judge*, on interpretation
of statutes, 101–102
Holmes, *Justice*
on child labor, 28
on clear and present danger, 84–85
on liberty, 80

Implied powers, 22
Indian claims, 6
Interstate commerce, 19, 36 (*see also*
Commerce clause)
federal power over, 20–25
Interstate compacts, 51–52
Interstate reciprocity, 52–54
Interstate relations, 49–54

Jackson, *Justice*, on military power over
civilians, 72
Jaybirds, 101
Judicial activism, 3ff, 80, 102
Judicial passivism
"deference," 4–5
doctrine explained, 3
presumption of constitutionality, 3
Judicial power, means of achieving
constitutional goals, 5
Judicial questions, distinguished from
"political," 18
Judicial review
congressional sanction, 2, 13
constitutionality of, 2
and democracy, 4
by federal courts, 2–3
of federal statutes, 2
of political questions, 14–18
as positive force in government, 2
power of Congress, 12
and racial discrimination, 102
by state courts, 3
of state statutes, 3
Judicial supremacy, controverted, 10
Judicial system, 46–48 (*see also* Dual
court system)
Judiciary Act of 1789, 13
Justiciability, 6, 14–18

Law, as machinery, 1
Law-making power, national
interstate and foreign commerce, 19
tax-levying, 19

Law-making power (*cont.*)
vs. state, 19–21
Lend-lease, 69, 71
Libel of government officials, protected
as free expression, 90
Liberty, interpretations of, 78–81
Liquor, in interstate commerce, 36
"Literacy" tests, 102
"Litvinoff" assignment, 69

Military government, 71–73
Military power over civilians, 67, 71–73

Necessary and proper, interpretations of,
21–22, 41–42, 68
Negroes, rights of (*see also* Civil rights;
Discrimination; Segregation)
constitutional protection, 93–95
education, 97–99
judicial interpretation, 93–96
racially biased juries, 94–95
suffrage, 93–96
discriminatory legislation, 101–103
New Deal, federal power under, 30–32

Obscenity, 83
Ordinances, constitutionality of, 7

Police methods
exclusion of evidence, 107–109
and right to counsel, 106–107
"Political questions"
categories, 14–18
defined, 15
doctrine, 17–18
distinguished from judicial, 18
Presidency
"stewardship" theory of office, 61–62
textual foundations, 55–56
President
appointing and removal powers, 10,
56–57, 59–60, 63
as commander-in-chief, 56, 69
relation to Congress, 55–63
constitutional powers, 56–57, 61–62
delegated powers, 58–59, 68
development of powers, 57–58
enumerated powers, 56
executive privilege of non-disclosure,
60–61
foreign relations power, 56–73
and Supreme Court, 63
veto power, 56
war power, 70–72
Presumption of constitutionality, 3